The Practitioner Handbook

The Practitioner Handbook

For Students of *The Science of Mind*

Second Edition

Mary E. Schroeder with Dr. James Golden

Authors Choice Press
San Jose New York Lincoln Shanghai

The Practitioner Handbook
For Students of *The Science of Mind*
Second Edition

Authors Choice Press
an imprint of iUniverse, Inc.

For information address:
iUniverse, Inc.
5220 S. 16th St., Suite 200
Lincoln, NE 68512
www.iuniverse.com

ISBN: 0-595-20687-5

Printed in the United States of America

Dedication

This second edition is dedicated to over 2,000 Science of Mind Practitioners around the world who used this book in its original form. Although it wasn't perfect, the first edition found an eager audience from Nigeria to Russia to Canada, and all across America. Six years after its initial publication, it continues to be used by churches affiliated with Religious Science International and United Church of Religious Science, Unity, Divine Science, and dozens of independent churches. This second edition is only being published because of your continued requests. I honor you for your commitment to this most profound teaching.

Mary Schroeder

Contents

Preface

The Science of Mind curriculum for Practitioners, commonly called Third Year, was a real mystery to me as a Second Year student. There wasn't much information available about how it worked or what was taught. The comments I heard most related to all of the reading.

Shortly after I found Religious Science, I knew I wanted to be a Licensed Practitioner. The principles of Religious Science made an immediate difference in my life; I could not learn enough about the teaching. Whatever there was to learn in Third Year, I wanted it. To me it was an important step and meant further progress on my spiritual path.

On the first night of class, we were asked to write down answers to a few questions: *What will Third Year be like?* I replied: Fun reading, challenging reading, and a lot of reading. I expect good discussions, but wonder how much of it will be over my head? *How much will I grow?* Don't know or I'd already be there. Imagine it will be a lot. *How will I grow?* In ways that will enable me to help others, yet at the same time I expect to stretch and reach into the deeper aspects of me. *What do I want out of all of this?* I expect to be trained as an intern practitioner, able to ferret out the cause of someone's pain, to be more powerful in my own life, more compassionate and powerful at work, and centered a greater part of the time.

The last night of class these cards were returned to us. My, oh my, Third Year was all of this and more. And, as I found out when I began, it is difficult to explain.

Mary E. Schroeder, R.Sc.P.

The primary activity of life is the activity of mind seeking wisdom, which is mind inquiring into the nature of God.

Benedict de Spinoza

This handbook is meant to supplement the classes and work of Third Year students and is not purported to be a complete teaching program.

Introduction

DECLARATION OF PRINCIPLES OF SCIENCE OF MIND

We believe in God, the Living Spirit Almighty; one, indestructible, absolute and self-existent Cause.

This One manifests Itself in and through all creation but is not absorbed by Its' creation.

The manifest universe is the body of God; it is the logical and necessary outcome of the infinite self-knowingness of God.

We believe in the incarnation of the Spirit in man and that all men are incarnations of the One Spirit.

We believe in the eternality, the immortality and the continuity of the individual soul, forever expanding.

We believe the kingdom of heaven is within man and that we experience this kingdom to the degree that we become conscious of it.

We believe the ultimate goal of life to be a complete emancipation from all discord of every nature, and that this goal is sure to be attained by all.

We believe in the unity of all life, and that the highest God and the innermost God is One God.

We believe that God is personal to all who feel this Indwelling Presence.

We believe in the direct revelation of Truth through the intuitive and spiritual nature of man, and that any man may become a revealer of Truth who lives in close contact with the indwelling God.

We believe that the Universal Spirit, which is God, operates through Universal Mind, the Law of God.

We are surrounded by this Creative Mind, which receives the direct impress of our thought and acts upon it.

We believe in the healing of the sick through the Power of this Mind. We believe in the control of conditions through the Power of this Mind.

We believe in the eternal goodness, the eternal loving kindness and the eternal givingness of life to all.

We believe in our own soul, our own spirit, and our own destiny.

We understand that the life of man is God.

Chapter 1

Now We Begin

Great teachers throughout the ages understood the Universe to be the result of the contemplation of Divine Mind, which created mankind out of Itself. Our individuality is a consequence of the thoughts of Divine Mind formed into images. Therefore, as God expresses through us (the result of Its consciousness), we become more conscious of our own divinity. The teachings of Jesus describe the Universe as a combination of love and law, of person and principle, of feeling and force. The Science of Mind philosophy is just as direct and clear.

> *The study of the Science of Mind is*
> *a study of First Cause, Spirit, Mind,*
> *or that invisible Essence, that ultimate*
> *Stuff and Intelligence from which*
> *everything comes, the Power back of*
> *creation—the Thing Itself.*
>
> *Ernest Holmes*

The beauty of this process is that we live in a spiritual Universe of pure intelligence, perfect life, dominated by love and reason, and the power to create. It may seem confusing because we are individually subject to the effects of race consciousness to the extent that we buy into it. (These are widely held beliefs found throughout society, along with our accumulated personal life experiences.) As our personality unfolds, we can consciously create our desires on the outer with the use of inner thought. Our conclusions and assumptions thus become part of the relative cause of our outer experience. By learning and practicing this teaching, we bring higher levels of understanding and truth into our consciousness, which lawfully out-pictures in our experience. This concept can be understood intellectually, but the greatest experience in life is to use it, thus the gift of becoming a Science of Mind Practitioner.

The ability of the medical profession to heal the soul is impossible. They are primarily focused on healing the effect, the physical problem, without any concern for the original cause. Billions of dollars are spent each year destroying diseased tissue, removing growths and unwanted things in the body. In time more of this energy will be focused on the real cause, the mental cause that lies behind all unhealthy conditions. As people search for answers to the visible cruelty and hardships in the world, a renewed effort has surfaced that searches for answers on the spiritual path. Subconsciously all people seek to return to unity with God. It is inherent in our nature. Jesus implied there is also a higher purpose to illness in the body, which should not be equated with spiritual health, because the two are not perfectly tied together.

Spiritual healing is based in rediscovering truth, being in touch with the wholeness of the Universe. It is finding inner peace, that special contact with God that is always there but may be temporarily hidden from view. It is possible to feel the presence and power of God and through that peace find harmony in the body, relationships, work, and prosperity. Since the Presence is always there, grace and joy unfold in life only in proportion to our recognition and acceptance of it. It is useless to sit back and wait for God to make its presence known—that work is up to us.

The unconscious feeling that there is good available to each one of us and we ought to have it, is permanently part of the makeup of human beings, according to the teachings of Emma Curtis Hopkins, a famous spiritual healer in the late 1800s. She felt this feeling lived within every human being and provided a tremendous source of strength. To her, the word "good" had a special meaning—the search for good as actually a search for God. In her work, she taught students the value of telling the truth about their good so it would appear in their life. She recommended being truthful about what you want, putting away any and all ideas that could interfere with it.

Meister Eckhart, a 13th century German mystic, saw the mind as easily controlled by fear, which at times temporarily satisfies itself by holding onto superstition. Yet, over time he felt the basic human need was to think freely. He believed the craving for right action (which Emma Curtis Hopkins called good) would eliminate fear and overcome even the most stubborn superstition. Three centuries later, Giordano Bruno, an excommunicated Dominican monk, proposed that moral conduct came natural to mankind. He saw goodness as a fundamental impulse of the soul and encouraged every person to experience life fully.

Goodness and unity are key to this one undivided spiritual system that never expresses itself in fragments. Parts of God are not literally scattered about the Universe. If the Universe is perceived as divided, the belief in duality will mentally create the illusion of separateness from the Source. This separation manifests in undesirable ways, which perfectly reflects and expresses the Law of Cause and Effect. An effect always mirrors Cause, the image of our consciousness: an impersonal, neutral, receptive and reactive law. It is a mechanical principle like any other. If you are dishonest in life, dishonest people may show up in your life. If you are not truthful, people may lie to you. If you are confused, you will end up in confusing situations. The law operates irrespective of personal opinions. But when you turn back to oneness through Spiritual Mind Treatment, you are again aligned with the power of God, the power of good, and the attributes of light, love, life, peace, power, beauty and joy.

There is disillusionment along the spiritual path for many people because we come to find out that:

* This is it, God is not going to come and save us because God is all there is and is already everywhere present.
* Change is continual and the less we get upset about it the easier it is.
* The purpose of the game of life is to play the game.

Is the work difficult? Not if the divine grace of God is allowed to operate in us, as us. It is possible to effort and worry every step of the way, but if we let go and allow the nature of the Universe to be our guide, life will unfold sweetly and more beautifully than anything that could have been anticipated. When the rush of everyday life obstructs your good, it is Spiritual Mind Treatment that shifts consciousness and brings you back into unity with the Source. Therein lies its power.

Growth is an endless force in all that occurs and, like a magnet, pulls all people towards God with no conclusion or final revelation. At all times the law of the Universe pulls us towards the recognition that God is in everything. Meister Eckhart wrote that God is not just the good things in life, because all of life is God. At times progress on the path to a higher consciousness can seem very slow, but there are no limits except the ones we place on it. These principles are in operation at all times and the outer demonstrations in life clearly show at what level we understand this. We are all IT—the express manifestation of the infinity of God, and individually we have the opportunity in this lifetime to discover it.

Spiritual wisdom starts the day that
we know from now on every discovery
is either a discovery of the self or related
to the self in the Cosmic Mind. The self
must raise the self by the self.

Ernest Holmes

Religious Science understands human misery to be the result of ignorance of the Law of the Universe. It is awareness of our divine nature that frees us from ignorance and all its effects. Anything that helps in this pursuit of knowledge to overcome suffering without negatively impacting others is good. The purpose of the Science of Mind philosophy is to teach the nature of reality, make it personal to everyone, and then to use this *power for good* for definite and specific purposes. Making use of the law to change your life's experience and perceive the ever-presence of God **is the only reason for studying it**.

Our whole practice and theory is based
on the assumption that the visible and the
invisible are just as Einstein said about
energy and mass: equal, identical, and
interchangeable.

Ernest Holmes

Therefore, it is Intelligence that moves, since that is all there is. The Intelligence of God has created all and it operates on the principle of law and order. Why? We will never know. How? It can never be fully explained. It just is the way it works. Using affirmative prayer, called Spiritual Mind Treatment, the Universe receives your thought and creatively acts upon it. The effectiveness of a treatment depends on the clear thinking, logical affirmation or arguments, and realization of the Practitioner in establishing First Cause.

It is wishful thinking to imagine being able to do a treatment and eliminate all of the problems in life. The experiences of life seem to be in confrontation with and divert attention from our true nature, undermining inner peace or destabilizing health or relationships. If these effects are not given power, they will not have any power. There is only one power in the Universe and the Science of Mind Practitioner works constantly to stay in that knowing. To the degree one knows and accepts the truth, is the degree to which treatment will succeed. The Practitioner looks at disease, sickness, or any other form of ignorance confidently knowing it has no power. Nothing prevents the principles of a God-centered Universe from manifestation except our recognition of it. It is Truth that sets the Practitioner and the client free.

> *I don't believe our movement*
> *is worth a dime unless*
> *something happens.*
>
> *Ernest Holmes*

The Practitioner is a teacher of Truth and offers their understanding of this Truth to clients so they may recognize their own divinity and turn from having faith **in** God into having the faith **of** God. As a teacher, the Practitioner carries a light into a darkened room; through treatment, truth is revealed. In this way the room and the mind of the client will then remain illumined.

Now We Begin

QUESTIONS FOR DISCUSSION

1. Explain the Science of Mind principle: We believe in God, the Living Spirit Almighty; one, indestructible, absolute and self-existent Cause.
2. What is Universal Law?
3. What are the differences between a medical doctor and a Practitioner? Does a client deny the benefit of one if they use the other?
4. How would you explain what the mental cause of illness means?
5. What is meant by rediscovering truth?
6. What will life look like when a client rediscovers God?
7. How can we know the difference between ego and intuition/Spirit?

READING SUGGESTIONS

A Legacy of Truth, pages 31-58
Bible Mystery And Bible Meaning, pages 203-220
The Anatomy of Healing Prayer, pages 1-40
The Art of Spiritual Healing, pages 11-72
The Edinburgh & Dore Lectures on Mental Science, pages 1-47
The Law and The Word, pages 1-17
The Science of Mind, Sections 1-4, pages l-60
The Science of Successful Living, pages 1-43

Chapter 2

The Concept Of Spiritual Mind Healing

We live in a Universe of pure intelligence, perfect life, dominated by love and reason and the power to create. As we evolve, it is our own conscious cooperation with the laws of the Universe that move us forward. Every form of matter is Spirit and the intelligence of the Universe is in the essence of every one of its manifestations, regardless of form. The individual intelligence in each person is able to use this truth to fully express itself in terms of freedom.

The Laws of the Universe are always in operation, but so much of the time they seem hidden and we are generally ignorant of them. It is being conscious of our life experiences, both positive and negative, that lend insight to these laws. We can tap the benefits of the laws we come to understand, knowing that they are not personal, but universal. Doubting the operation of Universal law eradicates its benefits.

Spiritual Mind Treatment is the art and science of inducing thought within the mind of the one doing the treatment, which perceives the life of the client as a Divine, Spiritual, perfect idea. Spiritual Mind Treatment is affirmative prayer, spoken in a scientific manner and in faith. It is a statement placed into the Law, embodying the concrete idea of our desires and accompanied by an unqualified faith that the Law works for us, as we work with it. Prayer or treatment is the alignment of our individual thought with the perfect right action of God.

Treatment is not something one does to another, nor to a situation. It is always the thing one does for oneself. Treatment is an action in thought alone. It opens up avenues in the mind, expands consciousness and lets reality through. Spiritual Mind Treatment involves deliberately inducing constructive thought within the medium of Universal Mind, which in its creative function as Law tends to produce in the outer world an equivalent of our inner thought. It is an art, a skill that can be learned and taught. It is an act, something that is done, and is not done until you do it. It is a science, a technique that operates in accordance with definite Law.

Five Steps in Spiritual Mind Treatment

1) **RECOGNITION**
   God is the source of all, the unlimited power.
   GOD IS…

   Declare your definition of God in many ways.

2) **UNIFICATION**
   God acts through me, as me, in me and all life.
   I AM…

   Declare your spiritual nature, the reality of all people in many ways.

3) **DECLARATION**
   I initiate my life experiences through my thought. I now choose my desired experiences.
   I ACCEPT…

   Declare the truth about the person in the here and now. Go from the general to the specific. Deny each symptom and affirm the Truth for each.

4) **THANKSGIVING**
   I joyfully accept the now present activity of Law acting through my intention perfectly.
   I GIVE THANKS…

Declare the work is already done.

5) **RELEASE**

   I release any doubts or concerns as I let go and let God, "the Father within", do the work. I now feel and act as if it were so.

   Declare a strong statement of love and truth, releasing it to the Law.

AND SO IT IS!

Spiritual Mind Treatment is not faith healing or a "get rich quick" scheme. It recognizes that God is all knowing (omniscient), all powerful (omnipotent), and everywhere present (omnipresent). Energy and mass are equal, identical, and interchangeable, therefore treatment is effective when we know that God responds, God will always be there, and God is within. This is the perfect expression of unity. There is no difference between the mind and what the mind does. Truth cannot be confined to a definite space and time. Treatment or affirmative prayer is technically a nonlocal event, not confined to a specific moment or place. It operates outside the present, in the infinity of space and time. It doesn't go anywhere, but is present simultaneously everywhere. As Troward explained, Universal Intelligence is everywhere and there is a corresponding responsiveness hidden in each person's nature ready to be called upon.

> *The subjective mind is the creative faculty within us, and creates whatever the objective mind impresses upon it; the objective mind, or intellect, impresses its thought upon it; the thought is the expression of the belief; hence whatever the subjective mind creates is the reproduction externally of our beliefs.*
>
> *Thomas Troward*

Dr. Craig Carter referred to it this way, "Consciousness may be called the atmosphere of our awareness. The content of an atmosphere determines the life it will sustain. To change the conditions of that life, the atmosphere must be changed." Therefore, the atmosphere in our mind is critical to how we feel and experience life.

When Jesus talked about how to pray, he said to believe you have what you want and you will receive. **It is the nature of the Universe to give us what we are able to take, at the level of our ability to receive.** It cannot give us more; it has already given all. If we don't experience it, we have not yet fully accepted the greater gift. Each individual state of consciousness taps the same source, but each person has a different level of receptivity, thus the multiplicity we see throughout the world.

Health is defined as a condition of wholeness or freedom from defect or separation. To heal is to make whole or bring back together that which has been separated. It is a process of taking the client to an honest place of self-discovery so that recovery will last and conscious spiritual growth can continue. Healing is uncovering and erasing false images and thoughts that we have accumulated, letting the true perfection of the Universe reflect in our conscious mind. As we rush toward God, God rushes toward us with the Universal power of good.

> *Treatment, in its proper content, is the time, process, and method necessary to the changing and redirecting of our thought, clearing the thinking of negation, doubt, and fear, causing us to perceive the ever-presence of God.*
>
> *Ernest Holmes*

The value of being a Practitioner is the gift of seeing perfection, knowing there is nothing to heal, only something to reveal. The value for the client is that the Practitioner's belief in Spirit is greater than the client's belief in the necessity of undesirable conditions.

> *What you think, you feel;*
> *what you feel, you do;*
> *what you do, you become.*
>
> *Dr. Tom Costa*

Unpleasant and undesirable conditions could not remain unless there was a person/body/spirit present to create and experience it. The purpose of Spiritual Mind Treatment is to determine First Cause, the true issue from beyond the perceived problem, and then to affect change in the consciousness of the one doing the treatment, so that the undesirable condition will disappear. How fast can this happen? To the degree that the Practitioner accepts Spiritual Truth, it is instantaneous in its demonstration. The process of healing is the time, effort, and depth the Practitioner undergoes in the realization of Truth. **True healing is healing the cause that produced the effect.** Psychic healing may produce a change in effect, but won't change the cause, leaving it to produce other effects. Why does it work this way? The greatest minds do not know. Like any law, we just accept what is known about how it works. In the view of Ralph Waldo Emerson, our power is within ourselves, as well as the authority to use it. He felt not only do we have a God-given right to independent thought and action, we have an obligation to exercise it. Fear, based on ignorance, is our greatest obstacle.

A treatment session with a client is not about change, it is about realization. It is misleading to tell a client that through treatment they can have whatever they want. Theoretically it is true, but it is frustrating for most people since the result may not take the form they expect or anticipate. In truth they CAN HAVE whatever they CAN ACCEPT. This is why so much of the work is going beyond ego. If a Practitioner believes their work is with the ego, that in itself is belief in duality. The work is to recognize ones divinity and oneness with God; to raise the veil of consciousness, which keeps us from recognizing and accepting our own perfection.

We are not depending upon chance
but upon the Law. The responsibility
of setting the Law in motion is ours,
but the responsibility of making It
work is inherent in its own nature.

Ernest Holmes

Part of the spiritual process is to keep redefining the ego and the goal of life. Ego desires to get life organized, then stay put so the rest of life is easy. Ego debates what it would cost to demonstrate or get something. The result can be a great arrogance if the person ends up working only with ego and law but without God. When we get to the point where we are not infatuated with "things", we have found the secret.

It is the Universal-consciousness that enables healing to take place. It is the conviction in the Practitioner's mind that the client is completely perfect and whole. Evil has no power in itself and cannot be perpetuated in the face of truth. The negative effects are a result of a misunderstanding of truth. If we focus on the effect, the sickness or disease, it remains as it is. Nothing can be done to heal the condition until we recognize it as an illusion, a veil that has covered the true nature of God manifest as this person.

> *Spiritual mind treatment consciously used, is a definite and persistent and consistent attempt to think straight and logically, basing the assumption on a concept of an undivided and indivisible spiritual Universe here and now, and translating everything into the terms of Mind in action as law, and conscious intelligence as directive power.*
>
> *Ernest Holmes*

The Concept Of Spiritual Mind Healing

QUESTIONS FOR DISCUSSION

1. Explain the Science of Mind principle: This One manifests Itself in and through all creation but is not absorbed by Its' creation.
2. How do you explain the concept of unity?
3. Explain three ways to describe the five steps in Treatment.
4. Why do we say the Universe is perfect life, full of love and reason?
5. What are the Laws of the Universe?
6. How do you explain time and space?

READING SUGGESTIONS

Bible Mystery And Bible Meaning, pages 221-254
The Anatomy of Prayer, pages 41-90
The Art of Spiritual Healing, pages 73-92
The Edinburgh & Dore Lectures on Mental Science, pages 48-61
The Science of Mind, Chapters 6, 7, 8, pages 106-148
The Science of Successful Living, pages 89-103
Your Handbook for Healing, pages 1-22
Your Mind Can Heal You, pages 1-21

Chapter 3

Thoughts On Investing In Life

By Dr. James Golden

Everyone wants to be a millionaire, but few people want to do what it takes to get there. Many people want beautiful yards without mowing the lawn. We want delicious meals without washing dishes. We want wonderful children that grow up strong, healthy, and successful without the challenges of being a parent. We want the reward without the effort. Isn't it amazing how much time we spend investing in things vs. the time we spend enjoying the reward! The fact is, most of our time is spent in investment. If we don't enjoy investing, we limit our level of happiness.

How easy it is for the simple words of a friend to lighten our heart. Hearing someone say "thank you" can totally change our state of mind. When a parent tells a child how proud they are, it enhances the child's level of self-esteem. When we feel appreciated by others, there is incredible gratification and reward. The point is, it doesn't matter how much money is in the bank or whether we have a new car; fulfillment and love do not come from other people or outside circumstances.

By drawing upon spiritual qualities, we can increase our sense of happiness and fulfillment. Investing energy and time in our spiritual nature improves the quality of life. It fills that inborn desire for peace, contentment and love. Recognize that everyone wants life to be harmonious and blissful, but spiritually speaking, to do this we must stop judging by appearances. When we say we can only feel love if..."if" means we are judging by appearances. When we are spiritually aware, we don't need someone saying they love us or are proud of us. It is the love of Spirit, the all-originating love out of which everything is born, that is of any importance. This is God, our true nature and the nature of all people. We see those who are not aligned with this love, but it is within everyone none the less.

I signed up for a program at a meditation center recently and was excited about expanding my spiritual experiences. I arrived early and was asked if I would help wash some pots and pans in the kitchen. I was happy to help, since as you give you receive. I figured I had half an hour before the program started, no problem. There were 1,000 people expected at the session and cooking for that many meant there were a lot of pots and pans. The regular washer was not there, so a day's worth of pots were stacked up. There were so many, I had to push piles out of the way just to open the kitchen door. No problem, I thought, I could do some and then go to the program. After half an hour, the leader asked if I could stay longer so they would be ready for the next meal. I agreed to wash for 15 more minutes, but then this negotiation was repeated shortly thereafter. Finally, I decided to stay until all of the pots were done. Eventually the last one was washed and dried. I walked out to the meditation program and everyone was gone. Was I angry! I thought it wasn't fair, since I had come hundreds of miles and missed the whole program. Then the thought entered my mind that since I really didn't have anything else to do, I might as well put the pots away. As I stored pot after pot, I was hit with a bolt of energy. All of a sudden I didn't want to be anywhere else in the universe. The kitchen felt like heaven, like God. It overwhelmed me with a sense of how right it was.

My heart opened and I wept. Later one of the leaders came in to check on me and I stood there in this huge kitchen and said, "Bring on the pots!" This was the experience I came for. Funny, I thought it would come in the lecture hall. I clearly was having a more powerful experience of God then I could have imagined right there in the kitchen. God does move in mysterious ways. And it is so much more fun than predictable outcomes.

Chapter 4

What is a Practitioner?

A Practitioner is a person who is trained in the art, science, and skill of Spiritual Mind Treatment. Licensed to practice professionally, a Practitioner is bound by a high code of ethics to respect a client's confidence, and is dedicated to the cause of helping others. Going inside, a Practitioner gets clear about a client and their desire to change, so that the One Mind in which we all live and move and have our being, will work positively in the client's life.

Practitioners are unique individuals and do not "look" any particular way. Typically they love life and are curious about it. In *The Power of Decision,* Dr. Raymond Charles Barker wrote, "We are the means by which earth becomes heaven." We were not created to be average. Our life experience is self-made. This talent, unique to each of us, is to be used successfully or unsuccessfully—that is our decision. Immanuel Kant, an 18th century philosopher, taught that we lift ourselves up and out of ordinary experiences by raising our minds to extraordinary ideas and then learning how to put them into practice. He believed there were four great questions in life that wise people seek to answer: Who am I? What am I? What can I do? What can I know? This is the path of a Practitioner.

By using Spiritual Mind Treatment, a Practitioner demonstrates principle. **Learning how to align with Spirit and demonstrate principle only comes from personal experience.** No one can teach this, only our self experience. We cannot have a corresponding realization for a client beyond the level of realization within ourselves. That is why Jesus said if the blind lead the blind, they will both fall into a ditch.

> *A practitioner must not be depressed by depression or elated by elation. We must not be confused by confusion. It is only as we stand above and beyond them that our word has any power over them.*
>
> *Ernest Holmes*

The purpose of being a Practitioner is to deepen one's own consciousness and connection with God. A Practitioner must have a strong commitment to "go to God" and serve others. This longing helps the Practitioner to do clear treatment work and in truth know that **the longing for God is God**. This allows inspiration to pull us through spiritual practices vs. allowing desperation to push us.

Never try to sell this philosophy. It is only by our use of it, how we live and act that people will become interested in knowing more about it. In meeting with a client, a Practitioner presents the Science of Mind teaching to the client and lets them decide if they want to accept it. Therefore, the Practitioner is also a role model. The people at church and those who come as clients are there to activate their own potential and are looking to the Practitioner for help in changing something in life. Benedict de Spinoza, a philosopher who lived in the 17th century, said our obligation to the world is not to solve all of its problems, but to refuse to be one of them. The job of the Practitioner is to present to the world one more honest mind with a loving heart who lives a productive life.

As your interest grows in becoming a Practitioner, recognize it means living by the golden rule of justice and fairness. Practicing unconditional love will open up your heart and increase your intuitiveness. Using foresight and wisdom will keep alive qualities, which will stimulate growth. When you come to see things in a state of joy and deep gratitude, all perceptions of limitation fade away.

Peace of mind cannot be found in the past or the future, only in the present. Your peace of mind adds to the consciousness of peace for your clients and throughout humanity. Each day should start on an inner basis, free of stress, full of health, and peace of mind. During the day be conscious of how you contribute to others losing their peace of mind. Live a life of humility; be humble, respectful, cooperative, peaceful, and never arrogant. This means perceiving and cooperating with the positive desires of other people. See and feel a need and, if possible, fill it in an appropriate manner.

When you are willing to meet the needs of others, your own needs will be met. Again the Law of Cause and Effect rules. Reading about the life of Albert Schweitzer may lend more insight to this idea. He founded and operated a hospital in Africa, devoting his life to healing others. He found the kind of freedom we all want through fearlessly pursuing his instincts, by rising above a life of struggle to do what truly pleased his soul. His philosophy was based on one vital concept: reverence for life.

The consciousness of Truth alone is the tool of a Spiritual Mind Practitioner. The three important qualities for spiritual mind healing are: persistence, flexibility, and patience, which allows the client to progress at their own level of acceptance. You cannot guarantee a client specific results in terms of effect, but you can guarantee that a new cause will create a new effect. Cause is the sum total of all beliefs and attitudes. The result of treatment is unpredictable so you are treating the spiritual person to allow their being to reflect spiritual ideas.

The Practitioner does not see themself as a healer any more than a mathematician assumes they are the principle of mathematics—yet both are trained in how to use the principles. When doing treatment, the Practitioner knows that truth is superior to the condition that is to be changed. This belief in ultimate goodness must be greater than any apparent manifestation of its opposite.

Being a Practitioner doesn't mean you are without your own problems or effects. The mark of a Practitioner is that you, l) take responsibility for your life, and 2) learn how to use treatment to address what needs to be changed within you. When you have a personal challenge, go back to the Declaration of Principles and figure out how to get yourself out of what you got yourself into. A Practitioner maintains the highest behavior under ridicule from others. Many people believe in darkness, so it is the Practitioner's job to reveal light. To be successful in spiritual mind healing, take time to see yourself in unity with the client, not separate from them. If there is a feeling of separation, it is your mind that needs healing. A Practitioner is consistent, not different with different people. Make the commitment to be yourself and be truthful with everyone.

Clients often don't want to or are afraid of choosing a new direction or option for their life. When people say they don't know what to choose, actually they want the Practitioner to choose. Choosing for them would not work. You can facilitate their choice through general suggestions but not specifics. The best part of an interview is when the client makes their own choice. Treat that the client knows the right thing to do. The art is to help them see and implement their own highest cause.

At one time or another, the Universe pushes everyone to a limit where they wonder what is really going on in life. Sometimes crisis is the only reason a person looks to the spiritual path for an answer, otherwise they might not. A Practitioner helps people recognize they are at the gate, the gate of choice where they can step into a world of greater good. The more clearly a client sees this, the easier it is for them to step through the window. That is the beauty and joy of being a Practitioner.

A brief overview of the requirements of interns and Licensed Practitioners follows. For detailed information, see Chapter 28—Requisites and Procedures for Licensing.

Integrity

Since the Law always puts the Practitioner's word into motion, you must have confidence in your own power. Your word must not be compromised with contradictory signals. The Law, which operates in perfect harmony and unity, since that would only create anxiety. Every doubt about how the Law works will create a negative reaction within the Law since life is always corresponding to your inner spiritual state.

To be successful, a Practitioner maintains the highest level of integrity. Integrity is holding your life in line with your moral code, with principle. When you act in accord with your true higher self, your actions, words, and thoughts express it. Integrity requires being honest with yourself most of all. That is why daily spiritual practices are so important; going to that quiet space within makes you confront yourself, what you are really doing and how you are living. Your life is what you have made it. It is a reflection of your inner self. Any sense of discomfort with what you are experiencing in your life should be looked at in relation to integrity. A Practitioner cannot wear a blindfold and pretend everything is all right when it is not.

We are challenged to living in principle again and again throughout our lives. To the degree you recognize how far in or out of integrity you are with principle, is the degree your life expresses harmony. It requires awareness at all times. By maintaining a life of integrity, not only do you empower yourself, but you empower everyone around you.

Values

Personal beliefs about what is most important, your belief in right and wrong, good and bad, are values and they impact every aspect of your life. Over time many values become unconscious and instinctively guide your actions and reactions. When you feel out of sync or in turmoil, it can often be traced to being out of integrity with your basic value system. Instead of letting this incongruity operate at the subconscious level, a Practitioner should periodically reassess both their primary values and value hierarchy. Values change and if your present behaviors don't match your values, it is time to modify one or the other to resolve the conflict.

Values are specific and emotionally charged, such as when to tell the truth, whether to give a full day's work for a full day's pay, be on time for an appointment, cheat on a test, etc. Often values are formed in childhood and are based on the environment you lived in and the role of your teachers and parents. As an adult, those values don't always serve your needs and should occasionally be evaluated. Values are motivating factors in life, so being out of integrity with values can drain your enthusiasm for things you love to do. There is nothing worse than having strong values tugging at you from opposite directions.

Periodically reflect on the highest values you hold in life. What are your top ten values? What values do you hold in areas such as relationships, commitments, love, the place you work, the type of work you do, your role as a parent, the health of your body, ways to have fun, methods of creative expression, the amount of money you make, etc. Does your life reflect living in integrity with your values? If not, change your actions or change your values, but get back in integrity with yourself and regain inner harmony.

Requirements of an Intern Practitioner

1) Approval of the minister.
2) Complete all assignments given by the minister.
3) All class costs paid in full.
4) Submit a Letter of Intent to the minister stating your intention, how the coursework was helpful, what gift you have to give as a Practitioner, and agree that you will abide by the standards set up by RSI. Submit this one week prior to a formal interview with the minister.
5) Personal interview with the minister.

Other activities a church may ask of Practitioners and Interns:

—Teach non-accredited classes.
—Treat daily for the ministers.
—Treat daily for the church as a whole.
—Do an occasional evening service or lecture.
—Hold seminars for church members on how to do treatment.
—Help with a ministry of healing, doing treatments on request.
—Teach an occasional class on The Essence of Religious Science.
—Assist at Sunday services.
—Lead volunteer on a team.
—Interns may be asked to choose a mentor from the Licensed Practitioner staff and hold periodic meetings with them during their internship.

Requirements for Requesting First Practitioner's License

1) Complete a minimum one year of training as an Intern Practitioner.
2) Permission of the minister.
3) Successful completion of the Practitioner's Practicum and all fees paid.
4) Application for license must be submitted within three years of the completion of SOM III or SOM I, II, III, or IV must have been reviewed within the last three years.
5) Completion of RSI First Practitioner's License Application, including five case histories and letters of testimony (three will be sent to RSI with the application).

RSI Requirements for Annual Renewal for Licensed Practitioners

1) Continuing Education as defined by the RSI Board of Directors. Current requirements are a minimum of 72 hours of RSI accredited classes in the practitioner's own church within the last three years preceding the request for renewal and submittal of RSI renewal form and current fee.
2) Permission of the minister.

What a Practitioner Does Daily

1) Spiritual practices to maintain a conscious spiritual awareness for yourself, your church and others.
2) Support the church through SEVA (selfless service to God) in volunteer activities and service.
3) Support individuals who seek your help so that they may see cause(s) at work that may be creating limitation or see opportunities to implement cause for new growth, success, new opportunities, etc.
    a) Teach the principles of Religious Science.
    b) Teach people how to do their own treatment.
    c) Know the truth for people.
    d) Express love, support, compassion and caring in a personal way.

What Is A Practitioner?

QUESTIONS FOR DISCUSSION

1. Explain the Science of Mind principle: The manifest universe is the body of God; it is the logical and necessary outcome of the infinite self-knowingness of God.
2. What does feeling separate from the client mean?
3. What are the qualities you bring to becoming a great Practitioner?
4. What qualities could hold you back or make it difficult?
5. What unresolved issues may impact your ability to assist all clients?
6. What are your greatest fears about becoming a Practitioner?

RECOMMENDED READING

Bible Mystery And Bible Meaning, pages 255-268
Legacy of Truth, pages 47-58
The Anatomy of Healing Prayer, pages 91-128
The Art of Spiritual Healing, pages 93-104
The Edinburgh & Dore Lectures on Mental Science, pages 62-72
The Power of Decision, pages 1-64
The Science of Mind, Chapters 9, 10, 11, 12, pages 137-180
Your Mind Can Heal You, pages 21-40

Chapter 5

Thoughts On Relating To Other People

By Dr. James Golden

In relationships we sense our greatest connection to God, yet sometimes we think relationships should solve our problems. Other times we think relationships cause our problems. Is it that somehow we don't understand? Maybe we've forgotten how to love others naturally and at the same time easily receive their love.

God did not create relationships to be difficult just so everyone would feel challenged. Yet it is not unusual to find people thinking if the other person would only straighten up or change, life would be great. Entire religions have been formed around telling people what actions are appropriate or inappropriate. To me it is the worst form of hypocrisy. If the nature of religion is to solve all problems with rules, we would all be in bliss. The intent of rules may be pure, but they are not the answer.

I believe the number one thing God gave all of creation is individuality. Two trees or two rocks are not alike. Two snowflakes are not alike.

Nothing in this world is alike. There are things very closely related, but everyone and everything is unique and special. We are not here to copy each other or ask someone else what we should do. The game of life is to figure it out for ourself.

Because we have free will, people are not always going to do what we think. One of the cures for a disappointing relationship is to stop trying to get people to change. From a spiritual premise, when people do things that make us uncomfortable, the work is in ourselves, not the other person. They should not stop being their unique self because we are uncomfortable. It is very obvious if you think about it. The solution is to change that part of our self, which thinks we have the right to judge the behavior of others according to our standards.

Our personality is a combination of beliefs, attitudes, and opinions. These have combined over the years to form the conclusions we have about love. People may say "You're a real jerk." Sometimes we think, "Yeah, yeah, you've got that right." How many of us have been told we are not capable of doing a job and a part of us believes it is true? Eventually we begin to accept the opinions of others. Then someone tells us we are wonderful and part of us knows that is true also. The spiritual truth is we are not those conclusions. Conclusions may govern what happens in our life, but it is not what we really are. We are unconditional love itself. So the things that happen to us everyday are what we believe about ourselves. That is where free will comes into play. We are whole, perfect, complete spiritual selves, always, no matter where we go or what we think. What determines our experience on a day-to-day basis is our belief. Nowhere is this more obvious than in relationships, since they are an outward experience of our belief about our self.

Relationships with people are governed by spiritual laws. Just like gravity and thermodynamics, the forces in the Universe are lawful. Gravity doesn't look at your behavior and then decide how to treat you. It treats everyone the same. Electricity treats everyone the same. You can be a saint or the worst person in the world and if you stick your finger in a light socket the same thing will happen because it is law. Since the Universe is lawful, relationships are also lawful based on our belief. We reap what we sow in thought, word, and deed. This works in all aspects of life.

There are two rules governing relationships. One is all relationships reflect back to us our belief about personal value, integrity, wholeness, and worthiness. Basically people treat us just like we have consciously or unconsciously decided we deserve to be treated. Some of our beliefs are healthy for us, but others are not. We all have some neurotic beliefs. It's not bad, it just means there is always work to be done. We are here to experience the fruit of that work, the love within which is our divine potential.

The second rule about relationships is we can only receive what we first give. Jesus said "As you give, so shall you receive." In a relationship giving and receiving is critical. The qualities we want to receive are the ones we need to give. If these qualities don't come back to us from a specific person, then they will come from someone or somewhere else in life. So, when we bestow our love on one particular person, that person may not love us back, but the love will come back through the channel that best serves us.

Where we get in trouble is when we think if I love you, you better give it back in this particular way at this particular time. Of course that doesn't work. The challenge is to give love freely. Then, if we pay attention, we will find love multiplies and comes back to us. This is the secret of the Universe. We are cosmic beings on this plane of existence in a human body and now the game is afoot, as Sherlock Holmes would say.

In the midst of everyday life many things happen. People say things and we react. Sometimes we forget that life is based on our beliefs and instead we have unbelievable expectations of other people. Expectations lead, more often than not, to unhappiness. The reason it is hard to let go of expectations is because we believe what others do or don't do will seriously impact us. By law, other people are not the cause of anything in our life. WE are the cause of experiences in our life. Our own beliefs and attitudes rule what happens to us. Other people are only the messenger of our cause.

A current folk saying is "Don't kill the messenger," meaning the messenger of bad tidings. It is useless to kill the messenger. When people bring bad tidings, such as I don't like you, I don't want you, or I think you're wrong, recognize spiritually those words are your own lack of self-acceptance. Subconsciously you are the one who did something that created a reaction that sent the messenger. You may not consciously know you have those thoughts about yourself, but they will be shown to you. The universe would be a cruel place if you could never figure out where limited thoughts and beliefs come from.

The amount of good in any of our relationships is our belief in how much good we allow ourselves to have. The opposite is also true. The amount of discomfort in relationships, the anxiety, stress, lack of support, also reflects our relationship with ourselves. All of us have heard some strange things rattling around in conscious mind like: "Who do you think you are to have a good relationship"? or "What's so special about you"? Well, we are the beloved one in whom God is well pleased, that's who we are. We are the precious cosmic self.

The long-term result of expressing more love in our relationships is we become happy. One way or another, all relationships show us that the purpose of human life is to enter into bliss. There are some teachings that say we should suffer now because it will make us better later. This makes no sense to me. My experience is the more I suffer the worse I get.

We have no right to tell other people how to live. To the degree we think other people must obey our rules, is the degree we will suffer. We have the right to choose who we want to be with and how we want it to be. If people are bringing out the worst in us, we have the right to choose not to be with them any more. This is the key to successful relationships. There is no reason whatsoever that we should have relationships that tear us down. Even if it is a relative, any difficulty is still a lawful reflection of our consciousness. All relationships should make us feel better because we help each other feel the nurturing goodness of love.

Chapter 6

Practitioner—Client Relationship

The most important step a client can take is to request the assistance of a Practitioner. The moment they take the step, the path of healing begins. Know at this point the client is open to hearing the truth and that when you meet, they will receive what they need.

The Practitioner looks at the effect in the client's life and works to identify the Cause. The Law of Cause and Effect says we reap what we sow, what we contemplate we become. The explanation the client gives of the effect will indicate where to begin looking for the error in belief, which is Cause. If life is not working on the outer, there is a misunderstanding on the inner that is not as visible as the effect. The fact that the effect is there is proof that cause exists. The Practitioner does not hold the discussion on effect for long; to focus only on effect could keep the client talking in an endless circle with no resolution. The discussion should dig through the layers, going deeper and deeper to root out cause. Don't stop until you get there. The ego doesn't want to look at cause and will put up defenses, but as you burrow in, going from the head to the heart, the dam breaks and cause is revealed. Often it is when the client stops talking from their intellect and begins to feel uncomfortable that emotions finally surface. Don't let them stray from this effort. Discuss, listen and teach.

Jesus taught that a mental attitude of faith arrived at through love can perform miracles. When the disciples of Jesus asked how to pray, He told them to shut out all appearances to the contrary, go within and make a request, believing they possess the object of their desire and disregard all appearances to the contrary. "Therefore I say to you, whatever things you ask when you pray, believe that you will receive them, and you will have them." Mark ll:24. We know this as the Law of Cause and Effect.

At a Practitioner workshop not long ago, Dr. Carolyn McKeown described what she called the LITT Process.

> **Listen**—with a desire to help the client.
> **Inquire** to discover what they really want.
> **Teach** them to be their own master, teaching principle when appropriate.
> **Treatment**.

At times it might help to ask the client about their understanding and vision of God. Some people believe in an angry or vengeful God, while others believe in a loving or maybe distant God. It may help to reunite the client with a God who may have been distant and get back in touch with the unconditional love God represents.

Judge Thomas Troward cautioned about seeing ourselves as an individual personality that ends where another person begins. This is separation and is a misunderstanding of principle. The Practitioner and the client are not separate in truth and so the Practitioner creates the opportunity for the client to decide to open up and remain in a conscious state of receptivity. This is important so the client feels comfortable admitting their belief and the Practitioner is open to offering the truth. With the barriers removed, the Laws of Nature take over. When a barrier is broken, a vacuum appears which means the client is open. Now the love and truth offered by the Practitioner can flow in. Eric Butterworth explains it this way in *The Universe is Calling,* "God's will for us is so intense, so continuous, that it even filters through our willfully closed mind."

It is your job as a Practitioner to focus on the nature of the client's life as Spirit which God has made manifest in total perfection. The work is to be an instrument through which God-realization occurs. We do not sit in judgment of a client or resolve the effect that has shown up in their life. There is **no** advice to give and **no** purpose in suggesting to a client a right or wrong way to do something. If the Practitioner gets caught up in anxiety, it only perpetuates secondary cause. Just open up and let the power of God do the work. Getting caught up in the drama of their effect may cause the client to be concerned about the Practitioner's abilities.

There is never a session with a client that is unsuccessful. You cannot be responsible for completely new effects in the client's life, because you do not know their level of acceptance, their receptivity to the concepts of truth. The client has a right to do life the way they feel is best for them, whether you perceive it to be good or bad. Trust is key to the success of a Practitioner. Know that your time with a client is working itself out in its own way since there is nothing in the Universe that could work against it. As Emma Curtis Hopkins taught, believe in the good. Doubting good leaves us only with fear—future expectations appearing real.

During the inquiry phase of the client meeting, know that the connection between cause and effect is there. Only say what you can see and not what the client should do. Suggest they look at choices and think about what could be the highest path. The Law of Cause and Effect says if they change one thing in their life, their whole environment changes. Change or moving beyond the problem may feel uncomfortable for the client if it requires leaving thoughts, people or places behind. Holding your meeting in a place that helps facilitate and support the client can make the shift much easier. Spiritually there is no reason for anyone to stay in a negative environment. It is a choice. As all Religious Scientists know, suffering is not virtuous. Emmanuel Swedenborg, a mystical scientist who lived in the

17th century, felt society encouraged us to believe our troubles are caused by what other people do or what happened in the past. He recognized that in order to make life easier, we spend a tremendous amount of energy trying to change other people and the past.

When doing a treatment over the telephone, let the client know that after you do a treatment, you will hang up. In this way you will not take away from the release in the treatment. When doing the treatment in person, do not "hang out" with the client after the treatment otherwise the subject will come up again. Let the treatment sit with the client so they can hold it in their consciousness.

Payment Issues

The work of a Practitioner is a licensed professional service. Recommended fees for service have been established by Religious Science International and United Church of Religious Science, but the services of a Practitioner are never withheld because of an inability to pay. It is customary that some form of compensation be given either at the time of treatment or in the future.

If pay is a problem for a client, spend some time discussing prosperity and the law. Financial success is one way Spirit expresses. Limitation, even in the area of money, indicates some error in thinking. Life is a perfect mirror reflecting our thoughts, which include thoughts about prosperity. Since there is no lack in God, there is no need for lack in our lives. We are surrounded by Infinite Intelligence and can demonstrate monetary supply through right thinking.

Many people lament that they have to spend their days making money in order to meet their financial needs, and feel that their spiritual life must be compromised due to the time required at work. Many people also feel that God could not possibly be involved in the financial affairs of daily life. This attitude only succeeds in cutting them off from the potential of serving God through work and earning money.

The great saints know that God is in everything. Behind the myriad forms and guises of this world, the saints see only the unchanging Spirit, manifesting this infinite drama. Paramahansa Yogananda said, "Making money honestly and industriously to serve Thy work is the next greatest art after the art of realizing Thee."

Issues Of Confidence

In the search for Cause, the Practitioner expects the client to be totally open, honest, and willing to go deep enough to find the answer. This requires the client be vulnerable which may bring up irrational fear. Meeting with the client in a place that feels safe, is quiet and relaxing, where the client feels unconditional love and understanding from the Practitioner, is very important. Being entrusted with the deepest thoughts of a client means there is mutual respect. Honesty and integrity define the relationship where confidentiality is its cornerstone.

There are unspoken expectations of confidentiality that must always be honored. Recognizing the client's right to privacy insures that they can share their most intimate thoughts and fears with you. The Practitioner must also maintain a high level of integrity to be worthy of the client's trust.

Counseling vs. Interviewing

It is the nature of humanity to help relieve suffering and pain. Our choice in the practice of Spiritual Mind Treatment must always be focused on the unity of the client with their true nature. If we stray and see the effects in a client's life as separate from their true nature, our tendency may be to try and "fix" the effect. This creates a sense of separation, a duality where a Practitioner could buy into the suffering. This can hold the client in the effect of limitation, dependency and helplessness.

During the interview, the Practitioner seeks to understand the effect going on in the client's life that they want to change. From this point, the Practitioner works to locate Cause, the error in belief that has made itself manifest. If the Practitioner gets caught up in fixing the effect, it is a slippery slope into the role of counseling. Ram Dass recognizes this compulsive reaction to fix the Effect in a client's life as a "toxic tension" which can perpetuate the client's suffering. He explains that this naturally compassionate part of our heart can get mixed up in a struggle between love and fear and show itself in misguided ways. We have all experienced pity, professional warmth, or compulsive "fix it" behavior in others as they resist getting involved in an unpleasant situation. None of this is helpful to the client.

To help those in need is indeed a
great privilege. But the blind cannot
lead the blind.

Ernest Holmes

By slipping into counseling, a Practitioner unconsciously forces the client to become a patient. In giving advice on how to work with the Effect, personal opinion can set in, blinding both the Practitioner and the client to the Truth. This is unfortunate because it ignores Cause, leaving it to continue manifesting problems. Working only on Effect helps the client hold onto the problem they want to get rid of. It is far from being compassionate because it maintains a sense of duality. When a Practitioner recognizes they are caught up in the effect of a client, it is time to stop and immediately do a treatment for clarity.

What the healer does is to mentally uncover and reveal the Truth of Being, which is that God is in and through every person, and that this Indwelling Presence is already Perfect. We separate the belief from the believer and reveal that which needs no healing.

Ernest Holmes

Legal ramifications are another reason a Practitioner avoids slipping into counseling. A counselor and a client establish a legal professional relationship that makes malpractice law applicable. Although ordained ministers have typically remained exempt from malpractice liability, since counseling is a function of their ministry, the Practitioner is neither a minister or counselor. Legally a counselor is required to both "exercise reasonable care" in practice and posses a minimum level of "special knowledge and ability." Malpractice liability exists when it can be proven that 1) a counselor owed a legal duty to their client, 2) the counselor breached that duty by failing to meet the requisite standard of care, 3) the client suffered some demonstrable and compensable harm, and 4) that harm was caused by the counselor's breach of duty.

Malpractice law requires counseling be done without harm or detriment to the client. A breach of standard care by a counselor is the determination of whether the counselor's instructions were suggestions or prescriptions for change. For spiritual as well as legal reasons, it is in the best interest of the Practitioner and the client to avoid the area of counseling.

Practitioner-Client Relationship

QUESTIONS FOR DISCUSSION

1. Explain the Science of Mind principle: We believe in the incarnation of the Spirit in man and that all men are incarnations of the One Spirit.
2. If the issue the client has come to you with is not one you have handled before, how do you help?
3. What are three ways to explain the Law of Cause and Effect?
4. What should the Practitioner do or say when a client:
   —wants to focus on the past or other people?
   —wants a guarantee of change and a specific new effect?
   —continues to have scattered thinking?
   —fears change?
   —does not know their purpose in life?
   —is argumentative?
   —has psychoanalyzed the problem to death?
   —is positive they cannot pay for the Practitioner's service?
5. How do you explain faith to someone who thinks they don't have any?
6. How do you reach a conclusion without counseling?
7. When does a Practitioner tell the client how to resolve their problem?

RECOMMENDED READING

Bible Mystery And Bible Meaning, pages 269-284
Legacy of Truth, pages 59-68
The Anatomy of Healing Prayer, pages 129-155
The Edinburgh & Dore Lectures on Mental Science, pages 73-92
The Science of Mind, Chapters 16, 17, 18, 19, pages 266-323
Your Mind Can Heal You, pages 41-62

Chapter 7

Thoughts On How To Fix Other People

By Dr. James Golden

In studying spiritual philosophy we begin to realize that everything outside of us, our job, relationships, or health, has a cause. It is the essence of any metaphysical teaching. Metaphysical means beyond the physical. So there is a spiritual inner cause for the things which appear in our life. This is also true for relationships.

For better or worse, our relationship with people is the depth or lack of depth of our spiritual understanding. We see as much wonder, beauty and joy in people as we see wonder, beauty, and joy in ourselves. That's the good part. But we can feel the hurt, anger, and resentment towards others and that, too, is part of our understanding. If we are interested in deepening a relationship and finding peace and harmony with someone, our job is to identify what it is in us that is like the part of the relationship we want to change and then change that part in us.

There is a golden rule in metaphysics on how to fix other people and it is very simple: Leave Them Alone. Don't worry about why other people do what they do. Sometimes we don't know why we do what we do, so how can we figure out someone else? It is a waste of time. It doesn't have positive results or make us feel any better. And the other person usually doesn't think much of our ideas or opinions either. Here is a quote that deals with this idea from a book called A New Religion. This is part of a chapter about western religion and the unsuccessful search for harmony and peace. "It is as though millions of people suffering from a painful disease were to gather together to hear someone read a textbook of medical treatment in which the means necessary to cure the disease was carefully spelled out. It is as though they were all taking great comfort in that book and what they heard, going through their lives knowing that they could really be cured, quoting passages to their friends, preaching the wonders of this great book, and returning to their congregation from time to time to hear more of the inspired diagnosis and treatment read to them. Meanwhile, of course, the disease worsens and they eventually die, smiling grateful hope that on their death bed someone reads to them another passage from that text. Perhaps for some a troubling thought crosses their mind as their eyes close for the last time 'Haven't I forgotten something, something important? Haven't I actually forgotten to undergo the treatment?'" That is a very perceptive understanding of the current state of most religions.

Our disease is that we think we are different than God. It is stated differently in various dogmas. All of the cures are valid, whether it is Hinduism, Buddhism, or Christianity. Yet we walk around telling each other about this wonderful cure we found while we slowly die of the disease. Some people think the answer is money. If I could buy different things or have more in my life I'd be happy. A lot of people have achieved this goal and are very satisfied for a while, but the next thing you know their beautiful home doesn't matter at all. It is the same old person with just different things around them. Various religions call this the Fall of

Man. The disease in life is looking outward for fulfillment instead of inward.

Swiss psychologist, Carl Jung, journeyed to India in 1937 specifically to argue with spiritual teachers over the proposal that ego must be dissolved in some undifferentiated collective mind. Jung considered this proposal eminently unsatisfactory. How can you ask yourself to kill yourself spiritually speaking? It doesn't work. But often that is what we hear from some spiritual teaching and we may try it one way or another, but it can't be done.

If we lines up historically significant spiritual leaders such as Jesus, Buddha and Gandhi, and could vote which one had achieved the highest spiritual goal, could we say they had no personality, no ego? Were they all exactly the same? It is very obvious that each one achieved integration and wholeness and was a unique being. They had an ego that was not compulsive or ran away from life; it was balanced between inner and outer. Their ego was a mediator between the source of truth and the practical everyday life of being human. If we try to destroy our ego to be more spiritual, we won't get anywhere. We must look in a different direction. The solution is falling in love with our self. Don't go out to get the ego, make love with it instead. When there is lack of harmony and we feel incomplete, the answer is not to feel threatened by the void, but to fill it with love. Be open to it and be the beloved one in whom we are well pleased. As that happens, the mind will open up and accept it. We want our ego to be as big as God. Rather than walking around with a need to fix others, it is far more efficient to make love to our self.

Chapter 8

Practitioner—Client Meetings

It is very challenging to work with a client without a face-to-face meeting.
If the client is serious about clearing up a difficulty they are experiencing,
a personal meeting is always preferable since much of what a client com-
municates is nonverbal. During the initial contact, explain how a treatment session works, beginning with a discussion about the problem, that
you will ask some questions in order to identify the cause and conclude
with a spiritual mind treatment. Be sure they understand the cost (no
charge by interns and the published fee by Licensed Practitioners). This
information helps the client relax and view the Practitioner as a professional. You offer a valuable service.

Client meetings should be held in a safe and quiet place, such as a
church, to insure minimal distractions. A home may be fine if there is a
place where the client will feel comfortable, preferably in a spot specifically designated for this work. If a client does not want to meet, probe to
find out how serious they are in resolving the conflict. It may be that they
are in a crisis situation and need help immediately. For others, they may
just want you to "do a treatment" or possibly some sort of magic, while
they do nothing.

not absolutely necessary

What's the issue?
What are their belief
systems about the
issue?

Location
cost
explain treatment

It is important to have an answering machine hooked up to your telephone so that a client can get a response in a reasonable time. Be very prompt in answering calls. This is a priority, but at the same time be practical, only emergencies need top priority. If your schedule does not fit with the needs of the client, recommend another Practitioner and make the arrangements yourself to minimize the hassle for the client.

As a professional, you may have to tell a client what they don't want to hear. This may create pain, but do not avoid it. See the client through the pain, allowing them to recognize the level of suffering bottled up inside. This is true compassion and true serving and why it is so important that the meeting environment feels safe and comfortable.

If a client is focused on someone else in their life who is in trouble, such as relative or a friend, the Practitioner helps the client release the loved one to their highest good. While it is not appropriate to do treatment for a third party without their request or permission, you can treat for the client regarding their realization about a third party. It is not your job to make their decision for them.

Process

Sit in close proximity to the client, from three to five feet away. Keep tissues easily within reach. Make sure they are comfortable. It is never necessary to touch the client. Ask why they have come and then watch and listen. So often a client will do to the Practitioner exactly what they are doing in their life that has created the problem. Stop them at times and clarify what you have heard, using statements like "What I hear you saying is..." If they are rambling and you don't hear any logical connections, ask them again why they are there and what exactly they want out of the meeting.

Be sure the process and the interview is done your way. If a client has a control issue, they may try to take control of the session. Pay attention.

Sit in a comfortable place. Don't touch them unless you know them well.

Everything you do with a client is part of the process, so recognize what they are doing from the start. What is their mechanism, their control drama? They'll give answers in the 1st ten minutes about themselves.

Health Problems

Working with a client with health problems or who is under medication can sometimes be challenging to the Practitioner. Here are a few ideas for those with special needs.

—When doing treatment for someone taking medication, continuing to take medication is their choice and when a doctor sees improvement, the client can make the choice whether to stop the medication.

—Assure the client that going to a physician doesn't invalidate or conflict with spiritual mind treatment.

—If the client is perceived to be ill and doesn't want to see a doctor, discuss the possibility that they may be in denial.

—Do not validate the choice made by the client regarding a doctor. The manifestation of the healing may actually be found in the relationship they have with medical professionals.

—Doing treatment for a client who is sick is okay. Both perfect health and sickness are true, yet incompatible. Do treatment knowing that physical healing is one way to demonstrate the power of treatment. In truth, we do not know what success looks like in the bigger picture.

Always remember, a healing that demonstrates can be measured. It is not the place of a Practitioner to give a client medical advice, or any type of advice. The goal, the appearance of the goal, and the seeker are one.

We have no judgement about meds, that's their choice.

* Don't say this. Ask if they're scared. Are they afraid of dying?

Death and Dying

Our belief is that God is changeless, yet the form that God takes is always changing. It is expressed as being unity that always exists in the midst of diversity.* Death is just another experience, a higher order of change. While we are use to slow change, death often happens quite fast someone makes the great leap. This may make it very difficult for a client to reconcile, release and let go.

In truth we died somewhere in order to be born here. Birth and death are the same thing when we recognize the multitude of ways God uses to express. Being human is just one of them.

When a client has a close friend or loved one who is dying or if they are dealing with the prospects of their own death, their reactions may vary, but overall people work through fairly predictable stages of emotion in order to cope with the situation. These include denial, isolation, anger, bargaining, depression, and finally, acceptance. In her book "On Death And Dying", Elisabeth Kubler-Ross says throughout all of these stages there is one constant factor that enables the person to keep moving through the process, and that is hope.

In "The Tibetan Book of Living and Dying", Sogyal Rinpoche says the two spiritual things we can do for the dying is to give them hope and find forgiveness. Guilt, regret and depression can overwhelm a dying person. A Practitioner can focus instead on their accomplishments and their virtues and help them find peace of mind.

Ernest Holmes taught "The will of that which is Infinite can never be finite." He believed that the will of God cannot be death because God is the Principle of Life and could not produce death without destroying Itself. "Death has nothing to do with life everlasting, and is but an impatient gesture of the soul, wishing to rid itself of a body no longer useful."

After the experience of physical death, we carry with us a complete subjective memory, which links our experiences as we express through our consciousness. Therefore, we are the result of what has been before. Why is this? We will never know. All that is important is that we are here in this life to express through the use of our body and mind. As we go from one experience to another through this life and the next, however it is expressed, we are continually carried forward. "God is not the God of the dead, but of the living." Matthew 22:32.

As a Practitioner, you may be working with a client who associates death with something bad, frightening, or as a punishment. Denial of the truth about death allows the client to avoid facing the reality of their own death. The way to help a client who is afraid of death is to explain to them through principle the importance of living while they are here. The purpose of life is self-discovery. "All that means anything is that while we live, WE LIVE, and wherever we go from here we shall keep on living."

Don't judge. It's OK where they are. I want to heal because I really want to heal. You've got to heal the fear before you can heal the disease.

Read Ch. 17 in SOM ~~left~~ about immortality.

Trust that the body + soul know what to do.

Practitioner-Client Meetings

QUESTIONS FOR DISCUSSION

1. Explain the Science of Mind principle: We believe in the eternality, the immortality and the continuity of the individual soul, forever expanding.
2. How do you show compassion yet ask or tell the client a truth they may not want to hear?
3. How far can you compromise on allowing distractions during a client meeting?
4. If a client suggests weekly or frequent meetings with you, what is your response?
5. How do you help a client make a decision on a medical condition, for instance, whether or not to have surgery?
6. When is it appropriate to relate a personal story to help the client see or understand what you are saying?
7. What do you tell a client that is frustrated that their aging and ill parent won't let go of life and die?
8. How do you explain the unexpected death of a child?

RECOMMENDED READING

Bible Mystery and Bible Meaning, pages 285-300
Healers on Healing, pages 115-144
How to Use the Power of Mind in Everyday Life, pages 1-33
On Death and Dying, pages 1-33
The Anatomy of Prayer, pages 156-183
The Edinburgh & Dore Lectures on Mental Science, pages 93-100
The Law And The Word, pages 85-102

The Science of Mind, Chapter 13, pages 183-189 and Chapter 23, pages 371-389

You Can Heal Your Life, pages 1-38

Chapter 9

Thoughts On Surrendering To Love

By Dr. James Golden

When we think that people don't love us enough, we believe there is insufficient love in the world and we believe in lack and limitation. Surrendering to love is finding that love is always present. There are a couple ways to understand this. One is knowing the love we receive from other people is no more or no less than the love we have in our heart. The spiritual law is, as you give you receive. This is true in every area of life. The Universe takes what we believe and reproduces it in the form of everyday experience. In this way life is a mirror that allows us to see what lies in the depths of our being.

On the spiritual path, what we seek is a greater awareness of the beliefs, thoughts, and attitudes we hold. If we feel love only when someone says "I love you," we play a game of always trying to meet someone else's criteria. This is limitation. By surrendering to love we let go of all criteria and realize that in order to experience love we must start where love begins, In us and all around us. Love never goes away, only we go away from love.

There are three ways to increase the amount of love we have inside. The first is to work with spiritual laws. If we don't have enough love in our life, then we are not giving enough love. The reason we experience a lack on the outside is we hold back on the inside. The second thing we can do is realize that we're the only one who can heal our life. There are an infinite number of support systems in our church and communities to help with self-healing. Medical doctors assist in a physical healing and spiritual teachers assist in the realization of truth, but basically we must individually do the work. Surrendering to love means realizing all people are lovable. If we don't feel it, what is blocking our love? Sometimes people seem to be the problem in life, but the spiritual truth is they are not. They are a messenger bearing the results of seeds we planted.

The third path to love is recognizing it is impossible to feel angry or demoralized when love is present, because love requires us to be happy. Happiness is an absolute requirement for love. What we need inside is the willingness to become happy when we are sad. There is a story about a king who was very wise. He wanted to know the secret of life, so he asked the court minister: "What will make me happy when I am sad and also make me sad when I am happy?" After months of research the minister came back and presented the king with a ring inscribed with these words, "This too shall pass." Yes, the greatest moment in life is going to pass as well as the most tragic moment.

An amazing thing happens when we surrender to love—our emotions begin to even out. We find we are more consistently in a spiritual state. We see that God knows what God is doing by means of us, even if we occasionally forget. The suffering in our mind evaporates when we accept that all things happen for the best. There is One Intelligence working through us and by surrendering to love, we embody the truth that life is good. In this way, we see God in everything.

Chapter 10

Identification of Effect

A Practitioner listens to the client's story about the negative effects in their life, knowing in Truth, it is just a shadow. The effect you see is a mirror or mental equivalent of its cause. In the "Power of Decision" by Dr. Raymond Charles Barker, he writes it is not the sun that causes the shadow (effect), it is an object, person or obstruction (misunderstanding of the Law) that causes the shadow. When the obstruction is removed, the sun shines once again. The sun was there all the time; it never went away.

When a client sees only a shadow, their back is towards their true nature; God's reality is not alive in their experience. Living in a shadow creates doubt and confusion, which may be what the client is exhibiting. A rule of thumb is that the client will do to the Practitioner what they are doing to themselves, i.e., indecisive, argumentative, avoiding, blaming, denying, etc. When you, as the Practitioner, are grounded in truth, you see the client's story as only a shadow, no matter how ugly it may appear. If you are not feeling grounded, you can easily get sucked into the story and all of a sudden feel indecisive and argumentative, avoiding the hard topics. Dedication to daily spiritual practices, as well as a treatment for clarity just before a meeting, helps guard against getting caught in the drama of the client. In Science of Mind, we speak to the adult, not the inner child. If you are in doubt that you are speaking with the adult personality of your client, clarify it with them.

The pain and suffering experienced by the client can be seen as a wake up call from God. The degree of pain involved may be the only thing that finally pushed the client to call you. The Practitioner has no judgment about the effects in a client's life. There is no reason to look down upon any soul's approach to God. Jesus said, "Do not judge according to appearance, but judge with righteous judgment" John 7:24. In other words, do not be confused by the conditions around you.

Karma is not fate; it is a consequence of cause and effect. For every action, there is an equal and opposite reaction. Our fate is not sealed. Change the cause and the effect will cease to exist. Thoughts and feelings are also effects. Cause can be changed up to the moment before effect. The Universe is flexible; it is we who hold tight to cause and effect.

A Practitioner needs to know the specifics of a problem—a general statement will not do, neither will the client's conclusion of cause. Question the client about what is specifically happening in their life including the actual names of people. This helps to bring their feelings about the events they are experiencing to the surface.

Leave names, details. It doesn't matter who the people are.

Some may not be a good idea.

Ideas for Identification of Effect

- What does the client want? *Conditional yes, but...*
- Ask for specific examples of the effect. *- General*
- Ask how they would prefer it to be. *No*
- Use active listening: I hear you saying... *yes*
- Pursue the emotional points—what is it about? *No*
- When you feel off track, ask the client again why they called you. *No*
- If the client goes off on a tangent, ask what it has to do with the problem. *Be careful how you ask. Gentle.*
- Identify false images and beliefs. *- No*
- When you hear a race consciousness statement: stop the client and ask where it came from and then identify it as a purely limiting idea. *- No*
- **Teach principles.** *No Peripherally* *Instead*
- Restate truths. *- No* *Do Treatment*
- Show the client how their choices were based on false truths. *No*
- ~~Repudiate~~ *Gently* any statement of lack, evil or limitation. *Yes*
- Stop and explore any "Ah Hahs." *yes*
- Paint a linear picture to recap the process of how wrong belief resulted in bad effects, and how the Law will respond positively to a new cause or belief. *-No*

Always be a student

It may be appropriate to use empathy with a client, sharing from your own experiences. If their problem was previously your problem, they might find comfort in knowing how you solved it and other ways it might have been solved. Be blunt and say what feels necessary. *In general, No*

It is okay to say the issue is something you have had to work on, so the client knows you connect with it, but DO NOT indicate that you currently

Stay on track. For my benefit let's get back to what we were talking about.

have the same problem, otherwise the meeting becomes two people with problems and no answer between them.

> *Problems are indications that something creative must be done in mind.*
>
> *Dr. Raymond Charles Barker*

Time spent arguing with a client is a waste of energy. When someone is argumentative, don't buy into it. Do your own treatment to know there is no resistance. Take everyone right where they are and build on the affirmative thoughts they already have. Employ their faith in the most simple and direct manner possible. Gradually point out that their faith in other things is built on the same principle you are using—that of nonresistance. Resistance is a lack of understanding. Voltaire, an 18th century philosopher, taught that bad ideas cannot survive open and honest scrutiny, just as good ideas always survive every type of repression.

After listening to negative statements from a client, the Practitioner is the first one who has to be healed. The entire sense of lack, evil, and limitation must be repudiated. As always, the Practitioner deals with their consciousness and not with the consciousness of the client. There may be indications that the client feels overwhelmed if they say things like "I can't do it all." This shows a belief in duality and a disconnection from the Source. In truth, know there is never too much to handle and the world is always in balance. Now is the time to release personal responsibility. (This also works for the Practitioner) Your duty as a Practitioner is to do the work and release the outcome to the highest good.

Time is also an effect, so don't get caught up if the client's problem is not enough time. Time can be used as a limitation, when in truth there is no time. The Universe, Spirit is timeless. Ernest Holmes teaches that God is not limited by form, and this includes time. This concept is reinforced by physicists such as Helmut Schmidt of the Mind Science Foundation, whose article "Can an Effect Precede Its Cause?" was published in the prestigious journal *Foundations of Physics* in 1981. He concluded "Apparently, present mental 'efforts' were able to influence past events about which 'Nature had not yet made up her mind.'" Physicist Nick Herbert, in his book *Quantum Reality*, said "The moment of the world's creation is seen to lie, not in some unthinkaby remote past, but in the eternal now." Dr. Larry Dossey, in his book *Healing Words*, says "The non-local view [of prayer] suggests that the mind cannot be limited to specific points in space (brains or bodies) or in time (the present moment), but is infinite in space and time; thus the mind is omnipresent, eternal, and immortal."

When the client hits an "Ah Hah"—a revelation, stop and let them explore it. If they start repeating "yeah, but..." be sure to stop and explore those areas for errors in belief. "Yeah, but" indicates the client is not ready to take what the Practitioner has to offer. If the client says "I don't know", "probably" or "maybe," know that somewhere in mind the client does know.

Money is a reflection of how a person feels about themself and their acceptance of limitations. Do they feel rich in life, free to be prosperous? If they feel abundant and free from worry about money, they have the mental equivalent of a healthy mind. There are many common beliefs about money, such as: there is not enough; too much causes pain and suffering; it is the root of evil; it is usually obtained dishonestly. If these ideas come up, they should be explored and the error in belief corrected.

Identification Of Effect

QUESTIONS FOR DISCUSSION

1. Explain the Science of Mind principle: We believe the kingdom of heaven is within man and that we experience this kingdom to the degree that we become conscious of it.
2. If a client reveals an effect that shows tremendous harm is being done to another person, what is the Practitioner's responsibility?
3. How long does the idea of karma follow a client?
4. Is it ever too late to change cause?
5. If the inner child of the client is the one you are meeting with, how do you reveal the adult?
6. No matter what you say the client replies, "Yeah, but…". What do you do?
7. A client wants you to fix their spouse or friend since they are really the one causing the client's problem. What would the treatment be for?

RECOMMENDED READING

Bible Mystery And Bible Meaning, pages 301-323
The Anatomy of Healing Prayer, pages 104-215
The Edinburgh & Dore Lectures on Mental Science, pages 101-107
The Law And The Word, pages 103-131
The Science of Mind, Chapter 14, pages 190-214
The Science of Successful Living, pages 44-58
The Power of Decision, pages 65-104
You Can Heal Your Life, pages 1-69

Chapter 11

Thoughts About Renewing Our Enthusiasm

By Dr. James Golden

The teachings of Religious Science are based on the premise that thoughts and beliefs are the basis of existence; the Universe is a spiritual system; our outer life experience is a result of what is in our consciousness; it is done unto us as we believe. Assuming all of this is true, it is important to know what we do believe.

As we make progress on the spiritual path, we may be impressed how far we've come, but there is still a long way to go. This should not be discouraging. Recognize that periodically we need to renew our enthusiasm for truth and light. For example, relationships are exciting when they begin, but after a year may feel very dull. A job may be rewarding for a while and then become routine and boring. Renewing our enthusiasm is important in every area of life so we don't become disillusioned. The spiritual path covers a lot of ground and encompasses more than one lifetime. Whatever we can do to gain a greater understanding will be worthwhile.

This brings us to spiritual practices. In the areas of relationships, work, or health, we often get lazy in maintaining enthusiasm. The same thing applies to spiritual practices. After a while we may find ourselves making less of an effort to do our best and instead, look for a way out, an easy way to get by. But life demands something more of us and the spiritual path is no exception. It is important to be disciplined in areas like relationships, work, health, creativity, and spiritual practice. In the end, all we have is our knowledge based on discipline. Knowledge goes with us for eternity and is the most valuable thing we have.

Meditation is a paradox on the spiritual path and yet it is one of the highest spiritual practices. It can be difficult to do because our mind resists letting go. Sometimes we would rather mow the lawn than meditate. Meditation asks that we let go of our normal state of mind and enter a deeper awareness. Why? The answer is the same in all of the great teachings—to reach a state of realization where we recognize God as all that is; we and God are one. So often our whole life experience seems to be based on duality, feeling separate from God. When we see everything and every person as part of God, including our self, we are correct.

There is a twofold purpose to meditation. One is to gain authority over our mind so our consciousness is clear enough to make corrections when it goes on a path of negativity and suffering. Most people have little authority over their mind. However, when mind says its time to be a martyr, we always have a choice of saying no. With consistent practice, meditation increases our power over mind and enables us to clearly, without effort, say no when it is necessary. The second purpose is to experience the meaning of the words "I am one with God." Experience is different from knowledge. Ideas without experience weaken under pressure. In the same way, spiritual ideas don't handle much stress until we have a direct experience of divinity. It is experience that gives us tremendous strength and enthusiasm.

I believe the reason we don't have more frequent experiences of the grace of God is because we are not looking in the right place. Think of

God as the bright light of a movie projector, our consciousness as the lens, and our life as the screen. The light goes on and the shape of our mind projects form onto the screen. In a movie, the light stays the same and whatever passes in front of it is what shows up on our screen of life. When we are confused why life is a certain way, all we have to do is turn around and look at where the image is coming from. If we are always looking out, we see a continuous chain reaction of thoughts forming in life. Meditation lets us look back at the source and realize our life is truly in our hands. When we see the light of God within, it transforms our mind; we feel more secure and calm. We feel valued and worthy and have the strength, courage, and enthusiasm to do what we need to do.

Sometimes we think if we were more spiritual our life would be full of money and friends. Being spiritual actually means we see life from a spiritual point of view, seeing harmony behind the chaos. In meditation we begin to see we are the cause of our experience and achieve the realization we can change patterns in our life that do not serve us. The purpose of the spiritual path is not to get something we feel we are lacking, it is to reveal what we already are.

If client is drama queen set appt for week later unless dire emergency

Chapter 12

Identification Of Cause

By the time a client has contacted a Practitioner, the cause creating the negative effect in their life can be very difficult to see correctly. Emotions distort the client's ability to logically think through to the solution even when the client is another Practitioner. Often their opinion is if the world changed, situations, people, or conditions changed, they would be just fine. Seldom do they recognize that the change must be made within.

> *A changed experience can only happen to*
> *a changed individual.*
>
> *Since the world responds by corresponding,*
> *all work begins and ends in the self.*
>
> *Dr. Raymond Charles Barker*

Whatever has caused the effect for the client, feel assured that it is a misunderstanding of truth, of reality. Judge Thomas Troward explained that all positive conditions result from the active presence of a certain cause, while all negative conditions result from the absence of such a cause. He said conditions, whether positive or negative, become causes in their own right and produce new conditions on *ad infinitum*. Conditions are not causes in themselves, but links of a chain that keep reflecting our beliefs. Effect will always equal its cause.

1st Cause		Relative 1st Cause		2nd Cause
Cause				**Various Results**
Mind	**→**	**Visible action**	**→**	**and**
Spirit				**Future Possibilities**

The first step in identifying cause, is recognizing that there is no room for blame in spiritual healing. The client has experienced the effect for reasons you may never comprehend, for a purpose that may be greater than you can imagine on the soul or universal level. The only weapon that can effectively be used to change cause and thus change effect, in every case, is truth, the awareness of God. When this contact with God occurs, grace flows and healing can occur. Delving into a client's past doesn't guarantee their future will be any better. All neurosis is caused by attempting to avoid legitimate pain.

Illness may be the bodies way of sending msg.

Say to body & Universe:
Got the msg
Gratitude for it

*First the whole train of causation is started
by some emotion which gives rise to a desire;
next the judgment determines whether we shall
externalize this desire or not; then the desire
having been approved by the judgment, the
will comes forward and directs the imagination
to form the necessary spiritual prototype; and
the imagination thus centered on a particular
object creates the spiritual nucleus, which in its
turn acts as the center round which the forces
of attraction begin to work, and continue to
operate until, by the law of growth, the concrete
result becomes perceptible to our external senses.*

judgment means blame.

Judge Thomas Troward

Socrates observed how frustrating it was trying to figure out why wicked people prospered. He noticed that people who made certain mistakes may be prosperous but have a sick body, while others have money problems and are very healthy, or have no problems at all but instead have rotten children. He could find no entirely accurate formula for linking a specific cause with a specific effect. All we know is that effect will always equal its cause.

We are all subject to race consciousness, a thought pattern that automatically operates in everyone. It bombards us in the media, through contacts with people, is embedded in what we are taught, and is absorbed by members of society unless it is consciously rejected. Race consciousness is not an individual cause, but can be found at such an acceptance level it becomes a choice. This can often be the case when a client is frustrated in achieving success. There is no need to fear God wouldn't support us in success, if in reaching out for our greater good, we let go of something

Judging - based on externals. Not always conscious. Race consciousness only effect you if you buy into it.

else. Instead, race consciousness says it is best to be mediocre and not stand out from the crowd.

When the client gets emotional, ask what it is about. You are getting close to Cause. Emotional outbursts such as crying are one way to know the client has touched that part that seeks to be healed. Stop and investigate what is causing the emotion, because you are almost there.

Persistent problems and patterns stem from behavior that was originally intended to help the client overcome a problem. It worked so well in other areas, it was repeated and eventually became a habit, a subconscious process. When the client realizes this, they may think it will be a difficult pattern to quit. Remind them it doesn't take long to establish a new groove in consciousness. Treatment will cut a new groove, a new road so the old one will be gone. When the ego believes things are being taken away, it is actually God shifting things around. Know for your client that the future holds more power, love, happiness, and satisfied relationships (which are all inner states). It is all available, but up until now it just hasn't shown itself in physical form yet.

All is love, the impelling force; and all is law, the execution of love. Remind clients that just doing affirmations, such as "When I…then I…" won't solve a problem. It must be full acceptance of the nature of the Universe. There is never a time when we are not moving towards God. It is the essence of nature never to be satisfied; so the business of life, the constant progression of life, is always evolving and is never finished.

Identifying the Cause of Health Problems

Health is normal and sickness is abnormal. All things respond to mind, including health. Just hoping to regain health is a delusion; it carries no authority because there is no serious emotional impact in hope. A person seeking health must decide to be well before any spiritual therapy can start producing results. The expectation of being well is the key. There are many people who cannot be helped or healed through mental means because they will not take the responsibility of making their own decision for health. The maintenance of health takes determination.

Although there are no foolproof examples of possible links between Cause (the subconscious belief the client is holding) and health (how it is expresses in their life), some patterns have a tendency to be related, such as:

Hate:	abscess, goiter
Anger:	bad breath, burns, fever, hemorrhoids, infections, liver, sprains
Fear:	addictions, anemia, apathy, excessive or loss of appetite, belching, body odor, cholesterol, crying, diarrhea, far and nearsightedness, frigidity, headaches, heartburn, indigestion, influenza, nervousness, ulcers, stomach problems.
Pride:	gallstones, knee problems

The Practitioner does not make a judgment about the health of a client. It is not known whether it is a good or bad experience for the client to have ill-health, nor do we know enough about the big picture to be able to judge, compare, or classify a physical condition. The Practitioner does not know the life's work of the client and whether perfect health would help them achieve that spiritual goal. The focus of healing is always on the mind in order to have a lasting effect, not on the form.

After a considerable amount of time, if identifying Cause seems illusive, explain to the client what you have observed at that point. Ask what they would specifically like treatment for and focus on that. It is not necessary to determine "why" the effect has manifested. The treatment will still be effective because changing cause changes results in one way or another. Let them know that after your meeting, if things become clearer,

you don't have to solve all of their problems.

there is always an opportunity to come back for another session. If you would like to be informed on how the treatment unfolds, indicate it (although contact is not made by the Practitioner, only by the client). Give the client a taste of the perfection of the problem and that it doesn't matter in the big agenda. The love of God doesn't pay attention to a specific problem—only as an individual can we perpetuate it. Show the client examples of how they could make it different by getting back into the river, into the flow of life.

Identification Of Cause

QUESTIONS FOR DISCUSSION

1. Explain the Science of Mind principle: We believe the ultimate goal of life to be a complete emancipation from all discord of every nature, and that this goal is sure to be attained by all.
2. What do you think are the two most prominent causes at work in most people?
3. What could possibly be the cause for: bankruptcy, getting fired from a job, arthritis, auto accident, breaking a leg, experiencing a perfect nurturing and loving relationship, financial success, a promotion at work?
4. What do you do when a client refuses to look at Cause?
5. What happens when a client refuses to acknowledge responsibility for an effect?

RECOMMENDED READING

The Anatomy of Healing Prayer, pages 135-166
The Edinburgh & Dore Lectures on Mental Science, pages 108-114
The Science of Mind, Chapter 15, pages 215-265 and Chapter 21, pages 347-356
The Science of Successful Living, pages 104-117
Your Mind Can Heal You, pages 63-85

Chapter 13

Thoughts On Treating For Health

By Dr. James Golden

Some people hold onto an old idea that our eternal nature, our soul, is located in the confines of our body. This is false. Our soul or spirit is much larger than the physical body; our body lives inside spirit. It is our individual essence that creates our physical body and our world. Everything on the physical plane is inside our spirit otherwise we could not see it. We see from the inner consciousness of spirit, to the outer, which is a reflection of our beliefs. Spiritual importance is thinking of spirit as small. What is really small and insignificant is physical creation in comparison. There is only One expressing uniquely through each of us, individualizing that which is universal. Like a wave on an ocean, the wave is unique and individual but it is part of a larger body.

To help understand this concept an analogy might be helpful. The First Cause of creation is God. Think of God as the beam of a flashlight. The next level of creation is our individuality, which is like cutting out a paper star and holding it in front of the light; the shape of a star appears on the wall of life. Remove the paper and there is just light. The shapes are the results of our subconscious beliefs, such as our values, our physical body, mental state, and experiences in the daily world. These are all shapes we have cut out of paper. Religious Science teaches there is an unlimited supply of paper and scissors; we have unlimited ability to change the shape of our life. One of the most important changes is to identify our self with God instead of feeling separate from God.

In the instance of health, we want shapes that are harmonious. It requires that we remember that when we judge others, we cut that shape out of a piece of paper. When we are judgmental, the universe shines the light on the paper of judgment and only hears "I am." Whatever shape our mind becomes, we become. It is a tricky game, but it shows that what we give returns to us whether it is grief, support, or compassion. A healthy mind realizes this dynamic and realizes planting seeds of ill will is counterproductive to our health.

Spiritual health is making no one wrong because everyone is just reaping the seeds they've sown, good or bad. The Universe is so trustworthy we don't have to worry. Our job is not to get involved in the negativity of other people. This is what Jesus meant when He said turn the other cheek. Don't look at what you don't want to become. Contemplate what you do want through visualizations, affirmations, and treatment. It is our choice to stay in a situation so if we stay, there is no reason to complain. The agitation we create in mind stresses the body and is the cause of all disease.

If stress remains long enough and goes deep enough, it can create a very unhealthy condition. Yet we should not blame our self for getting sick. I don't know anyone who hasn't had some challenge. Being sick, we are working out our consciousness, our area of growth, through our physical body. Growth is a process. However it out pictures, there is no reason to see it as wrong; at times it is natural for the healing to take place on the physical plane.

I often see people get angry with themselves and resent disease. This blocks their power to reach a new conclusion. Instead, be your own best friend. The power is the love we can give ourselves. In spiritual mind treatment, watch what mind says about other people. If we have thoughts we don't want to personally experience, do treatment and change the thinking. When you are sick, love yourself no matter what. Self-approval and self-acceptance are great healers. If forgiveness is needed, do what is necessary to forgive and let go. We're all spiritually innocent. Trust the process, move through the experience and let knowledge be revealed.

Chapter 14

Treatment Focus

The technique of Spiritual Mind Treatment is lifting the consciousness of the Practitioner into alignment with spiritual truth, recognizing the client as Spirit always in perfect harmony with the image and likeness of God. This is the place where there is no one to be healed, just something to be realized, which is the client's true spiritual identity. When reading the words of Jesus, He referred to doing a prayer of faith that would cause a creative law to reflect back to the one praying, the situation and conditions corresponding to their beliefs—it is done unto you as you believe.

> *Behind every condition is a belief,*
> *and if you can change the belief,*
> *you can change the condition.*
>
> *Dr. Craig Carter*

The Practitioner works within their own mind until they are mentally satisfied and their whole mind understands that the client is healed. When this point occurs, Cause has been uncovered and truth revealed. At this moment it is time for a Spiritual Mind Treatment. The focus of the treatment is only ABOUT the client. The goal is to reinforce the belief the Practitioner has about the client, while the results begin and end in the consciousness of the Practitioner. This is how Law is set into motion. All treatment must end in a realization or it is just a bunch of words.

Each treatment is unique to the client and is not to be used for anyone else. The Practitioner, like everything in nature, grows every day and is never in the same place in consciousness twice. Each treatment must meet the needs of individual clients. The Practitioner is the vehicle for the power of God, not **the** power of God. You are not the doer; God is the doer. Through treatment, the Practitioner opens their consciousness about the client and the truth and power of their Christ or Universal consciousness, and ends with a clear knowing about the client along with a personal sense of inner peace. There should be a new realization about God for the Practitioner when the treatment is finished.

The goal of treatment for the Practitioner is to stand back in consciousness far enough to see both sides of the person's being. The Practitioner is clear that change and truth are available without sickness and disease. Treatment works independent of the Practitioner. Even if the client's issue is the same as the Practitioner's, each one has a different cause. Treatment is not willing things to happen, but opening up an avenue within where it can happen:

> *A treatment is a specific Cause, placed*
> *in Mind. Having given the treatment the*
> *responsibility of the Practitioner ceases.*
> *At that instant the Law takes over and*
> *does the work. There is nothing further*
> *to do except to expect results.*
>
> *Dr. Raymond Charles Barker*

In Spiritual Mind Treatment, the client ceases looking for answers in the past and lets go of fear of the future. Treatment brings new cause into their world and with it, a recognition they are their world. The first treatment should do all of the work necessary to heal Cause, provided there is a complete realization by the Practitioner— a sensing, feeling, internalization. Treatment reunites the soul of the Practitioner with its Source. That is why there is a feeling of conviction and total trust. A treatment from the intellect of the Practitioner may be perfect in form, but will not be effective without these things. As Paul said, "Now faith is the substance of things hoped for, the evidence of things not seen." Hebrews ll:l.

Treatment

In saying a treatment the Practitioner invokes grace and spirit. It works to change Cause right at that moment. This changes the effect at some point in time. It lets ego open the door allowing grace to flow in. Verbal treatment helps reach the greater reality; ego mind opens up letting meaningfulness come through.

Treatment has nothing to do with trying to concentrate the power of God; it already is. In treatment we permit, not petition; are positive, not negative; reach out to freedom and bliss, where there is no tension or struggle; allow a relaxed acceptance. Actually the words are not as important as the sincerity of the one giving it. The deficiencies of how well a treatment works are not in the words of the prayer, but in the conviction of the pray-er.

The treatment should have everything in it to cover the case. It is the business of the Practitioner to untie every mental knot, yet this does not mean giving direction to the client. We do not channel energy. Our energy is the same as the clients and both are equally spiritual. There are simply different levels of awareness.

When using denial in treatment, be sure to say something like "All limitations fall away." Denial can be used to cancel a limitation the client has accepted and help them get their power back. If you use denial to take something away, be sure to replace it with truth. For clients with excessive negativity or depression, ask the client to share two to three things they are thankful for, and in treatment appreciate those blessings in their life.

A demonstration is a manifestation. We cannot demonstrate beyond our ability to mentally embody an idea. It does not depend on location, environment or condition, only acceptance and belief. In cases of trauma and severe suffering, know that suffering is not necessary. The soul of the client will know it is time to go on to other experiences and growth or it is time to get better. Know that the soul knows what to do to get better and continue on its path in this reality. It is the client's choice and love is present in either case.

Disease will be healed provided you find cause and heal it, providing the person you are working with wants to surrender cause. Disease without thought could not manifest. The Practitioner turns from the condition and contemplates it as it ought to be, never as it appears to be. Clients are spiritually perfect and disease cannot attach itself to spirit. Our spiritual being is constantly remaking our physical being.

Questions to ask if the goal of treatment is in question:

—Does this add to the client's ability to take action?
—Does it express a more abundant life?
—Does it take away from no one?
—Does it create no delusion?
—Does it express a greater degree of aliveness?

> *We must do our share in the work, and not expect God to do for us what He can only do through us. We are to use our common sense and natural faculties in working upon the*

conditions now present. We must make use of them, as far as they go, but we must not try and go further than the present things require; we must not try to force things, but allow them to grow naturally, knowing that they are doing so under the guidance of the All-Creating Wisdom.

Judge Thomas Troward

Treatment Focus

QUESTIONS FOR DISCUSSION

1. Explain the Science of Mind principle: We believe in the unity of all life, and that the highest God and the innermost God is One God.
2. What is more effective, verbal or silent treatment?

RECOMMENDED READING

How to Use the Power of Mind in Everyday Life, pages 34-59
The Anatomy of Healing Prayer, pages 167-190
The Edinburgh & Dore Lectures on Mental Science, pages 115-123
The Law And The Word, pages 168-208
The Science of Mind, Chapter 22, pages 357-371
You Can Heal Your Life, pages 103-148
Your Handbook For Healing, pages 37-39
Your Mind Can Heal You, pages 86-122

Chapter 15

Thoughts On How To Find The Good Life

By Dr. James Golden

If you investigate the spiritual ideas behind various religions, there is usually a common thread—hope, trust, or understanding that life is deeper than the details of everyday living. We have all had the experience of disappointment one way or another, such as in relationships or careers. We've also felt great when things exceeded our expectations. But after either experience, mind eventually asks what's next, what shall we do now? Will there ever be an experience that is so blissful it can never be surpassed? This thirst for bliss is a longing for something that seems very illusive, yet great teachers have said bliss is available to everyone. By bliss they mean something that is better than happiness, something out of our normal state of living, a divine experience.

We taste the nectar of bliss at the birth of a baby, the miracle of life. Bliss is often experienced watching a sunset on the ocean. Something within us cracks open and we feel life is good for no particular reason.

This is the feeling we yearn for and the spiritual path is about finding that place. Jesus said the kingdom of heaven is within. It is a place in consciousness, not a physical place; it is a state of mind. Love and depression are states of mind. Heaven or bliss are also states of mind, a place of awareness we reach in consciousness. Something in us knows that is where we belong, yet how do we consciously get there? All religions and teachings try to convey the road map to that place; but looking around the world we find on the surface it doesn't seem to have worked well. Religions have been around for a long, long time and many of their leaders and members do not follow the teachings. All religions say the same thing—with all of your heart and mind, love God, then take that love and give it to people around you. If people have heard this for hundreds and hundreds of years, why hasn't it had a greater effect? Is it that difficult?

In the Christian tradition, believers say Jesus is expected to come any day now and then things will get better. Hindus say if we follow the scriptures, make a pilgrimage to Mecca and pray, life will get better. Jewish people feel the savior hasn't come yet but when He does, it will get better. On the outside, every religion has their own miraculous cure for the ills of mankind. But if you look deeply into these religions, into their basic principles and beliefs, they really don't say that. If you read the Bible, the Koran or the Upanishads closely, they don't say just wait and it will get better. They teach that something miraculous has already happened. The fact that we exist and can make conscious choices is a miracle. The miracle of life is fully at hand. Miracles are the normal course of events. The healings of Jesus show He used the same spiritual principles that are available to everyone. God doesn't play favorites. Jesus said what He did we shall do and more. He said we and the father are one, that God has already given all to us. One thing that precludes us from experiencing this divinity is feeling we are not good enough the way we are—so we look elsewhere. The greatest teacher cannot walk one step for us. The progress of our soul is in our hands. As humans, we are one beautiful way God is expressing, and God sits back and loves it.

A student asked a great spiritual teacher why the teacher seemed so extremely happy and joyous while the student was not. The teacher said it was because he liked his life experience and the student did not. It is done unto us as we believe. On the spiritual path we are looking for the ability to recognize we are divine. There is no reason to wait. Start looking. Do spiritual practices, meditate, read spiritual books, take classes, talk with friends and teachers about spiritual principles. Do what is necessary to recognize the divinity within. We are all connected to the same creative power of the Universe. The only difference between us and the greatest teacher is the use we make of the same power.

No matter what we think about, all God hears is "I am." The whole effort of the spiritual path comes down to a simple understanding: use your mind not as a reaction to life but as a catalyst for happiness. Imagine the greatest spiritual being and know you are one. That is the right use of consciousness. The miracle is us.

Chapter 16

Teaching And Exercises For Clients

There are times when using an exercise with a client may get to Cause in a much more meaningful way. Here are a few ideas.

THERE IS ALWAYS SOMETHING TO BE THANKFUL FOR

For clients with depression or severe negativity, ask them to share what they are thankful for. Do this for three minutes with no stopping. Then focus the treatment on appreciation for these blessings. A shift in attitude can occur through gratitude.

THE PATH TO THE PRESENT

Ask the client to choose a part of life and describe what is happening in that area. What were five stepping stones that led them to this position. Ask them to meditate to a point of rest on these steps and then write a dialogue between themselves and that area of life. Look for insights and areas of mistaken beliefs.

ZEN CLOCK

Draw two circles on a paper. Use them as two faces of a clock. In the first one, segment the clock by the amount of time they spend doing necessary things in their life, such as working, sleeping, playing, exercising, or reading. Use the second clock face to segment the time we would rather spend on each activity. Focus on changing Cause so that they can create the effect of the second clock face in their life.

TRUTH MADE EASY

Getting the client back on the path of truth may be easier if they can identify areas in which they can contribute love to the world. Using a paper and pen, let the client list the many ways they could do this and then ideas on how they can make some of those things happen.

BE HAPPY

One of the easiest ways a client can increase the level of happiness in their life is to:

1. Decide to be happy.
2. Stop complaining.
3. Find things to praise.
4. Pay attention. When you start seeing negative thoughts in your mind or hearing negative words come from your mouth, change it at once to positive and creative ideas.
5. Begin doing something new and different.

EXPANDING INTUITION

Intuition can be strengthened by experience. Troward wrote that if, in spite of all appearances pointing us in a direction of conduct, if there is still a persistent feeling that we should not do something, more often then not we shall be successful following our intuition. Why? We may not have conscious knowledge at the time, but it is the Law of Attraction and our subjective knowledge that is at work. Ask the client to talk about times when they did not listen to their intuition and ended up with a negative experience. Discuss the benefit of meditation and how it allows that inner voice to surface. Ask how they might make more of an effort to hear that voice.

WHERE IS THE STRESS?

If the client is feeling unsatisfied and unfulfilled, but is not sure where the problem lies, ask them to indicate their level of satisfaction (high, medium and low) in the following areas, followed by the level of importance they attach to each one (high, medium and low). Need: sexuality, friendship, being loved, loving others, self-esteem, creative achievement, spirituality, respect of peers, excitement and challenge, quiet and peacefulness, security in work, an intimate long-term relationship. The areas identified as high importance and low satisfaction are the ones to look at in the search for Cause.

WHO AM I?

Each of us plays a number of roles in life such as friend, mother, father, aunt, neighbor, leader, etc. How we describe our relationship to each of these roles can be an indicator where we need to change. Too often we wait for people or things in life to change, but if we change, then those other things or people will also change. Ask the client to list all of the roles they play and attach to each of the roles an adjective that best describes their relationship with it. Those roles with negative connotations are the areas that need change. Through the use of principle and law, show the client how they can become the thing they want to demonstrate.

THE BODY AS AN INDICATOR OF MENTAL EQUIVALENT

The body is a spiritual idea and every part of it is significant. There will be times when a Practitioner can see a client's body reflecting back to them an area in need of work. Can the client translate the physical malfunction to a mental or emotional equivalent? Some of the mental equivalents include:

Arm	=	embracing or releasing a situation
Body total	=	the sum total of conscious and unconscious ideas
Ear	=	sensing truth and understanding
Elbow	=	changing directions
Eye	=	perceiving truth
Face	=	facing truth
Finger	=	grasping details
Head	=	knowing truth
Heart	=	power, love, joy
Knee	=	flexibility
Legs	=	moving forward
Lungs	=	taking in the knowledge of God
Mouth	=	praising and responding
Neck	=	flexibility
Stomach	=	digesting and assimilating or eliminating ideas
Thumb	=	grasping ideas for comparison

WHAT IS AN ATTITUDE?

An "attitude" often develops when a bad habit has continued so long that it turns positive personal qualities into negative ones. Again we can find pairs of opposites. Can your client figure out the positive expression, the truth, that is being blocked by any of these negative attitudes: blame, envy, fear, prejudice, selfishness, self-pity, jealousy, criticism, judgment, anger, inferiority, confusion, self-doubt, resentment, worry, guilt, procrastination, competition.

RELEASE AND LET GO

Sometimes we bombard ourselves with negative messages that block our ability to move forward. These are often in the form of "I believe I should..." or "I believe I must..." statements. Ask the client to list all of their 'shoulds' and 'musts.' Why do they feel that way? What has kept them from doing each one? If they accomplish a should or must, how would it make them feel? Does it still feel important? If not, release it and let go.

PATHWAYS TO BLISS

The Law of Giving and Receiving is always at work in our lives. If a client is focused on how they can receive, it may be useful to ask how can they give. Here are a few ideas on looking at opportunities to give:

How can I add more value to my immediate environment?

What small decision can I make today to increase joy and happiness for someone?

How can I be vulnerable in this situation?

What small gift can I give others right now to melt a barrier or break the tension?

How can I communicate more clearly to get the other person to understand me?

In what way can I give others more of what I need?

What can I say to let the other person feel valued and listened to?

In what way can I show someone I value them as a person?

What can I say to encourage others to be honest and ask for what they want?

How can I show someone I value their friendship?

In what way can I express my desire to encourage someone to be who they really are?

How can I encourage a friend to open up and allow their creative energy to flow?

How can I show others that just being alive can be a love affair with the Universe?

Teaching And Exercises For Clients

QUESTIONS FOR DISCUSSION

1. Explain the Science of Mind principle: We believe that God is personal to all who feel this Indwelling Presence.
2. How important is forgiveness in the healing process?

RECOMMENDED READING

Learn To Live, pages 221-256
The Edinburgh & Dore Lectures on Mental Science, pages 124-140
The Science of Mind, Chapter 24, pages 390-423 and Part 6, pages 507-567

Chapter 17

Thoughts On The Nature Of Justice

By Dr. James Golden

Our society is based on the idea that the universe is unjust and we have to look very, very hard to find justice. Our whole judicial system is based on imposing justice on injustice. From a spiritual point of view there are two models to look at in deciding whether the universe is just or not. The first model is found in mythology, it is God versus the devil. People that are good reunite with God in paradise and people that are bad go to hell and have a terrible experience for eternity. This is duality, which says God creates good things, but people screw it up and God just accepts it. Unfortunately some religions believe people will be rewarded when they die. Duality is the belief there is good in the Universe, but also a lot of bad.

The second model is the metaphysical idea of unity. In this model, God created by becoming the Universe. Since God is everywhere present and the only thing It can do to make something is to use part of Itself. The unity point of view is God is everywhere present spiritually but also literally. The Universe is created out of divinity. Individually then, we create our own experiences in the Universe which can only be perceived as good or bad because there are lawful rules that govern how it works. The main rule is very simple—we become what we believe.

In this Universe of unity, justice is at hand. It is always present because everyone reaps what they sow. In metaphysics we know nothing can come into our experience that we don't allow into our experience through consciousness or our subconscious. This is why it may be hard to grasp the significance of things like the Law of Attraction. Some think it is okay to attract prosperity, health, friendship or love, but if we attract someone stealing our car, the concept may be hard to believe. It gets very confusing, yet the spiritual truth is: the Universe is just. If God is everywhere present, how could there be injustice? Can injustice and God occupy the same space? My answer is no. Therefore there are two choices—God is not everywhere present and therefore injustice thrives or we believe God is everywhere present and what appears to be injustice is not at all.

If you know someone who lives in a world where injustice seems to thrive, it is the metaphysical meaning of hell. It is a place where things happen without apparent reason. Hell is that state of mind where it looks like we just got sick, ripped off, abandoned, or were taken advantage of. It is a mind that lives in torment. But in truth, it cannot be so. In the natural world any biologist will say nothing just happens. There is no such thing as a spontaneous event; everything is Cause and Effect. The natural world is so dependable airplanes don't have to be redesigned every week because the world of aerodynamics changed. The Universe is predictable. Every morning the sun rises in the east. Why should human life be different? The cause that creates events in our life begins within us. This also means that we are free, free to change anything.

All religions have said that mankind is deluded and does not see the truth correctly. There is a veil that blocks our view of the world as it is. In the East they call it maya, the illusion. When we think someone or something is responsible for what happened to us, it is illusion. This is not an experience of God. We experience our self as a farmer who opens his window and wants to know why pumpkins are growing when he planted corn. It is the world of illusion. In reality no one touches our field because it is a field of consciousness and no one is allowed in our conscience but us. We may think a lot of people are in there—mother, father, sister, teacher, boss, etc., the little committee that talks to us all the time, but it is actually our voice.

At times we look at war between countries and it seems like both sides feel they have the answer but the other side won't cooperate. Thousands of people can die; there is so much pain and suffering. At the same time, as many people that died at Hiroshima, die every day of starvation. Every single day they die and we hardly think about it. Death is so normal on this planet, but it doesn't have to be that way. It is a delusion that someone else is responsible for the problem, so we don't find the answer to meet the needs of all people on the planet. This is the essence of justice.

It is a spiritual commitment to believe that justice is done, that everyone is reaping and sowing, reaping and sowing. Whether we win the lottery or get mugged in the back alley, we are reaping and sowing. At the same time we don't condone acts of violence as just old karma. We don't need violence or suffering on the spiritual path. This calls for strength to remain sane and know there is no one in the field of our consciousness but us and whatever seeds we plant will be what we get. If we get what we don't like, don't blame someone else, talk to our self and say "Hey, self… what are you doing? How did I get mixed up and allow these things to happen? What am I going to do about it?

Events on the scale of war between countries reflect another dimension of human experience. They are dramas played by real human beings. Every single soldier is there out of their own consciousness. It is not right or wrong. We have in our own inner world evil rulers by right of our own consciousness. There is drama unfolding in world events, just as our individual lives get dramatic. Recognize there is a purpose to this drama and it will reveal something. The human race is trying to grapple with a new idea, the idea of world peace. It used to be that war seemed easy. The good guys over here and the bad guys in a country far away; it was okay to go to war. Now it is not always easy to decide who are good guys and bad guys. We see good and bad on both sides.

We can make the leaders of countries wrong when they go to war, but it doesn't solve anything. The question is how do we solve the problem of human beings killing each other? How do we solve starvation? How do we solve violence and crime? Assume the Universe is unjust and we'll never find the answer; we just cope until we die. If the Universe is just, then it is reaping and sowing, which means there is an answer to these problems. The next question is, what is it? What do we do? I guarantee when people like you and me have gone beyond the need to have war there will be no more war. It is just a bunch of people fighting. There isn't one person or president out there doing it by himself. It takes a lot of people. Not that any soldier or army is wrong, it is the evolution of human consciousness that we are dealing with. It is evolution and growth.

If we want to solve the problem of war, then we must start by solving the difficulties in our mind. We can't give what we don't have—a basic spiritual principle. All of us would like to give peace to the world. We would like to give it out by the handful. But we can't give what we don't have. The outer wars reflect the inner wars. How much anger, revenge, blame, and war-like consciousness is in each of our lives? Realize we each need to bring peace to ourselves first. If we can do that, then we have the capacity to give it.

During the Gulf War I received a letter from the President of Religious Science at the time. He wrote "The issues and problems in the Middle East are complex and there are many, many minds involved seeking the best solution. Let us use our minds to know the principle which makes all things new, to see to it the best possible decisions are made for the good of all and this crisis ends with a real victory for everyone—for everyone." It may be hard to think of victory for a country that may be considered the enemy. We tend to only think of victory in terms of our piece of the pie, but the spiritual solution does not favor anyone's point of view. It does favor the potential of human beings to express themselves.

We have a chance to do that now. Believe in the principle of God's presence so much that we are unafraid, even of war. Know for ourselves and all of mankind that something can be done. Our consciousness can be raised by opposing no one or no thing. Ernest Holmes said this teaching is against no one but for everyone. Know that God is everywhere present in all people and all things and that divinity knows how to solve it's difficulties. It is impossible for God not to be able to solve a problem. Whatever the difficulties, personally or collectively, there is an answer.

The highest use of spiritual mind treatment is knowing there is an answer. You don't have to know what it is, just that it is. It can be used on both a personal scale and a world scale. Look at what happened in Germany, the walls literally could not stand up to the consciousness. When the people changed, the walls came down. The role of intelligent, spiritual human beings is to believe in the answer more than the problem. Have faith, there is an answer to world problems. We must believe more in the solution than we do in the problem.

Chapter 18

Case Studies

#1

A church member was experiencing intense fear about her health. She had been suffering frequent arthritis pain, continuous infection of the mouth and chest pains brought on by emphysema. She was taking medication for stomach problems and sleeping only two hours a night. As her condition worsened, she was feeling a great deal of sadness and anger.

The Practitioner found Cause to be a lack of self-love and unworthiness. The treatment focus was on harmony and love, trusting the Law to achieving perfect health in its own way.

After treatment work with a Practitioner, her life really changed. She says, "I realized that I am not inherently evil, and I have nothing to fear. I am truly an individual, unique expression of God, Love and Good. The result of this sudden, dramatic revelation is that for the first time, I expect as much from myself as I do from everyone else. I came face to face with my doubts and fears, which were mostly about my health, and we met them head on with Truth and treatment."

She goes on to say, "Arthritis seems to run in my family and it was crippling all of us. My pain was getting worse than ever. On the day of the treatment work, I was in severe pain. I have had no arthritis pain since then. In addition, my chest is now remarkably free of pain. My sleeping pattern has gone from two hours a night to five or six hours."

Four months later, she is still pain-free and has no further need for the medications she had taken for years. A previously diagnosed ulcer has also disappeared. She also had a fungus infection on her foot, which was never discussed at the treatment session, and it has disappeared. Interestingly enough, exactly the same condition had been present on the Practitioner's foot, and that, too, was healed.

#2

A client sought assistance from a Practitioner regarding work and prosperity. He had been in and out of work, which was creating chaos in his family. During the interview the Practitioner found Cause to be a disregard for life as God in action. The treatment focus was on love as law.

After treatment, he reported, "Much to my surprise, I found out that my real need was for inner peace. After the treatment, I could feel a change in my consciousness, which amazed me. Later that day, a friend called to tell me about a job, but when I went in the next morning, his boss said that he couldn't hire me. Normally, anxiety and fear of lack of money would have taken over, but to my surprise, I was calm, content and peaceful.

That evening, another friend called me about work. When I showed up the next morning, his boss also turned me down. Again, I was calm and peaceful—not worried. That night, one of my friends called again and said I should come in the next day. This time, the boss hired me.

Throughout these three days of uncertainty, I was able to remain unaffected by these conditions. My mind automatically chose peace and contentment, even though I was completely aware of everything that was happening."

#3

A church member sought the help of a Practitioner because she was suffering a lot of pain over an old relationship. She was having extreme difficulty putting that person out of her mind. The Practitioner found Cause to be the fear of not being enough. Treatment focus was on being pure love and pure light.

After the treatment, she reported, "I have suddenly realized that I want to have a relationship with myself so that I can better understand my own thinking and emotions and avoid all the fear, hurt, and pain that develops when I move too fast in relationship. The really great part about this experience is that I am seeing a change in my thinking. I am aware of my feelings, yet I am making conscious and rational decisions about what I want to do. The pain over my prior relationship has gone away."

As Dr. Ernest Holmes wrote, the healing process—insofar as it may be termed a process—is in becoming conscious of the Eternal Truth: our lives are none other than the Life of God.

Case Studies

QUESTIONS FOR DISCUSSION

1. Explain the Science of Mind principle: We believe in the direct revelation of Truth through the intuitive and spiritual nature of man, and that any man may become a revealer of Truth who lives in close contact with the indwelling God.
2. Why in Case #l did the Practitioner also have a healing?

RECOMMENDED READING

The Edinburgh & Dore Lectures on Mental Science, pages 141-155
Questions And Answers On Death And Dying, pages 1-38
You Can Heal Your Life, pages 195-204
Your Mind Can Heal You, pages 163-176

Chapter 19

Thoughts On Dealing With Depression

By Dr. James Golden

Psychologically speaking, depression often means being quietly angry with ourselves rather than vocalizing our thoughts in the world around us. We lament our condition, are unhappy with circumstances, relationships or worse. Because we don't share our problem with others we get depressed. The classic experience is being a martyr. We have to take the trash out when no one else wants to. We wonder why the other person doesn't care. We feel we're not getting paid enough at our job. We feel stuck in a relationship and see no way out. The martyr always seems to be self-absorbed, not totally aware, and has a certain quality of depression.

What is really important is our spiritual level of awareness. If we can heal ourselves at the spiritual level, the psychological level will take care of itself. In any emotional or mental experience there is always one of two causes at work: doubt or fear. Doubt or fear are the root of every single limiting condition that a human being experiences. Both can be overcome by going back to the truth of God as everywhere present. Spiritually, depression is really resistance to change. Being depressed on a spiritual level means we are putting on the brakes and refusing to take a positive step in consciousness. Think of it as being on a sailboat in the middle of the ocean, headed for a place we really want to go. The wind comes up, the sails are set, and we throw out the anchor.

Sometimes we are unafraid and fearless, willing to face challenges, at other times we aren't conscious of our resistance to stopping the fear. The easiest way out is to become depressed. Then no longer are we fearful, we're just angry and upset. When we feel depressed, one of the first questions to ask is what am I afraid of? The logical part of mind doesn't ask what's it afraid of, it says we don't like something and we're angry about it. If we look deeply, fear is the root cause. Elimination of fear is what spiritual mind treatment is all about, healing our mind of its indulgence in doubt or fear.

Recognize that change is inevitable, no matter how much we dislike it. It is also called impermanence. No matter how bad things are they will change, no matter how good things are they will change. No person of any spiritual caliber has ever wanted to stop change. The most wonderful or the most terrible relationship is going to change. If you have a lot of money or no money, it's going to change. Change is not always from good to bad or bad to good, but it is a constant process of things moving around.

The Universe is a creative process in constant motion. Sometimes we think of creation too literally such as believing all things were created in the past and now things are unraveling. More accurately, creation is an ongoing process happening every moment. Each day is a re-creation, a new day. This moment is the re-creation of a previous moment. God is constantly at work with the same creative power that made the world out of nothing. If there wasn't an ability to create anew, we would be sitting on the floor because our chair would disintegrate. When we hit the floor our body would dissolve; if it wasn't for re-creation our body would not hold together. All the cells and molecules would disintegrate. There would be nothing but a void without creation every single moment.

Creation means change, so as re-creation continues, things get into different relationships with each other. It was God's desire that manifested all of us, so we are God's different forms and guises interacting with Itself. God doesn't make reruns. God experiences Itself anew every single moment. Change is one of the things that God is. The only choice we have is giving some direction to what change takes place, but not the fact of change itself. One of the first things to do if we feel depressed is look closely and find what we are resisting. If we indulge in martyrdom, hurt or self-pity, we won't find the thoughts and strength needed to heal the depression. Instead we'll find more pity and anger. What are we resisting? What is the change that is so scary we don't even know what it is? When we recognize what it is, depression leaves if we get busy and deal with it. The important thing is to look at depression and use the wisdom of our consciousness to find out what it is and then do something about it.

Too often people try to hold onto things which inevitably create suffering. No matter how much we love someone, that person will die; we can't stop it from happening. That is the bad news, the stuff suffering is made of. It can also be looked at as an adult temper tantrum. Like a child that stomps its feet and yells when it doesn't get its way, adults do this by saying we are going to be unhappy and make others miserable until we get our way. Lots of luck. Depression is very ineffective. The reality is we can change and bring about new circumstances without being so self-indulgent. First, let go of the old way. Face the fear of loss, of losing that which we are afraid to lose, which is not always physical things, but includes beliefs or ideas. For instance, if the person we are dating finds someone else, depression won't bring them back. Instead, realize there is a way to positively respond to that change. Our emotions are valuable messengers, but at the same time emotions are not good advisors. If we always followed our emotions, we'd all be in jail. The appropriate response is to decide what to do and face the change. It could be as simple as altering the image we have of ourselves.

Every religion says we should not judge by appearances. We think this means don't be judgmental. But there is a deeper meaning which does not appraise a situation based only on circumstantial evidence; don't reach a conclusion on anything based on the evidence of our five senses. If that is all we rely on, most of the appraisal will be wrong. Beneath the surface of conscious mind, there is only one intelligence working and it knows what it is doing—changing, evolving, and growing.

Ernest Holmes said in order to grow on the spiritual path, see through the condition and find truth. Growth is like taking off a tight pair of shoes. It is the resistance to growth that is painful. Change is never bad; the resistance to change causes tremendous suffering. When we find ourselves in resistance, we can go in the opposite direction—the direction of surrender, which is trust and faith. In the Bible, when Abraham was asked to sacrifice his son, he had unwavering trust and nonresistance. He was absolutely dedicated to doing what God asked; then God spared the son. This is the model for surrender—faith and conviction. The symbolism is absolute conviction and trust, to have faith in God even if seems like the worst possible thing God could ask. In the story what looked like the worst thing turned out to be the best, because after leaving the mountain, God gave Abraham a huge kingdom where all his people would be happy. The ultimate reward was given and Abraham was able to expand his faith and belief among thousands of people as the reward. The reward was far different from what it looked like in the beginning. In the same way we experience doubt and fear, we are in the same position as Abraham, being asked to do something beyond our perceived ability. The spiritual idea is to trust and know we're in the right place for change to happen for the best. It is God working through us to bring about a new and greater idea.

And so my recipe for dealing with depression is to, 1) love our self in spite of everything else. Forgive our self and honor the growth process. 2) Let other people help. Self-pity is really just a temper tantrum. Indulge in the feelings and then seek the company of people we trust. Share how hard it is and let them love us. It is impossible to be depressed when others are helping. 3) Love God even when God seems unresponsive. In the midst of our struggles don't renounce God. Don't send our reality to hell.

I was in the car with two of our young children last week and they had picked up some new terminology in school. One said something and the other one said "Oh, God damn it!" I asked if they knew what they were saying. No, they just heard it on the playground and thought it was cool. I told them it meant they wanted God to take all of their toys and break them. They wanted God to come into their body and make it puke. They wanted God to take all their friends away so they would never see them again. That's what it means. And they said "Whoa! We take it back. We don't want that to happen." So think about what you are asking God to do if it isn't surrendering to divine reality. Watch where the mind is going. Rather than traveling down the path of pain and suffering, ask God to bless reality and show the way to change. Be willing to do whatever it takes with conviction so that it will all work out beautifully. Ernest Holmes put it this way: "Mankind has learned all that it needs to through pain and suffering." There is no need for more.

Chapter 20

Ethics And Professionalism

Fundamental to the success of individual member churches and societies is the credibility and integrity of the conduct of their ministers, leaders and Practitioners. As representatives of their churches and societies a high degree of ethical conduct and professional integrity is essential.

The policies of Religious Science International, including the RSI Code of Ethics for Practitioners, are established to govern the conduct of Practitioners in the area of ethical and professional conduct. Consequently, these policies are to be interpreted and applied by the RSI Board of Directors, and are not open to interpretation by individual Practitioners.

RSI Practitioners shall not support, encourage, promote, endorse, practice or teach anything which can be construed to mean: that The Creative Power operates beyond the consciousness of the individual; that more of The Creative Power resides in one individual than another; that The Creative Power is directed by any means other than thought. This is directed specifically toward any kind of support for or use of gurus, mediums or channelers who claim to have special spiritual wisdom transmittable only through them or special contact sources of wisdom unavailable to any individual through the use of his or her own consciousness. It also includes any kind of support for or use of any kind of inanimate objects such as crystals, pyramids, charms, or amulets as means of bringing The Creative Power into activity in the consciousness of the individual. It does not, however, preclude the discussion of these matters for educational purposes, providing that such discussions are not construed to be either promotion or an endorsement.

RSI Practitioners shall not, at the public level, make derogatory or critical remarks about the integrity or ability of Religious Science International, its elected or appointed leaders, or of any of their fellow Practitioners. This means from any public platform, including their church services or classes. This includes statements made on recordings or in writing intended for publication or sale. This is not to discourage complaints or dissent, but to encourage that such be addressed openly through legitimate channels.

RSI Practitioners shall not use vulgar language or offensive humor in making public presentations from their own or any other platform. What constitutes vulgar language or offensive humor is always open to interpretation, however, should the matter come up, the opinion of the RSI Board of Directors will be decisive.

ACCREDITATION

RSI grants Practitioner licenses to qualified individuals whose sole spiritual commitment is to the teaching of the Science of Mind and the practice of Spiritual Mind Treatment under RSI Policy and Bylaws and in service to RSI member churches.

Licensed Practitioners who seek or accept status of a religious or spiritual nature from other organizations are in violation of policy and their licenses are automatically revoked. This does not apply to credits earned in a fully accredited institution for courses in religion or philosophy.

RSI PRACTITIONER CODE OF ETHICS

Article I A Religious Science Practitioner operates under the authority and license granted by Religious Science International for the purpose of practicing and disseminating the principles of Science of Mind and acts in a manner reflecting such principles. The speech and conduct of a Practitioner always reflects the dignity of this high profession.

Article II A Practitioner's work is done "entirely in the field of mind," the highest use of which is Spiritual Mind Treatment.

Article III A Practitioner's Treatment is complete in and of itself, therefore the Practitioner does not suggest more than one Treatment. Additional Treatment may however, be requested by a client.

Article IV A Practitioner complies with all state and federal laws.

Article V A Practitioner does not counsel or give advice.

Article VI A Practitioner does not solicit a client.

Article VII A Practitioner does not denigrate the work of another Practitioner.

Article VIII A Practitioner does not knowingly accept a client who is simultaneously a client of another Practitioner without consent of the other Practitioner.

Article IX The relationship between a Practitioner and client is one of confidence and trust and is held inviolate. The private affairs of a client are never divulged, nor is a case discussed in a way that would identify the client.

Article X A Practitioner does not refuse to do a Treatment for a client who is unable to pay at the time, but treats for the client's demonstration of supply.

Article XI A Practitioner advertises by personal card, listing in a church bulletin, RSI Publications, yellow pages in the telephone book, and New Thought Quarterly only. An announcement in the local paper with wording acceptable to the pastor or sponsor is acceptable.

Article XII A Practitioner financially supports and actively participates in the ongoing growth of the church and is supportive of its pastor. A Practitioner is also supportive of Religious Science International.

Ethics And Professionalism

QUESTIONS FOR DISCUSSION

1. Explain the Science of Mind principle: We believe that the Universal Spirit, which is God, operates through Universal Mind, the Law of God.

RECOMMENDED READING

The Edinburgh & Dore Lectures on Mental Science, pages 156-166

Chapter 21

Thoughts On Selfless Service

By Dr. James Golden

Spiritual practices tune up our mind just like we tune up a car. Since reality is greater than what we see on the surface, by being spiritually tuned up, we don't get attached to things. If someone rejects us, it can be easy to get stuck being anxious and unhappy. If we are criticized, our mind may get attached to our negative aspects awhile. Being spiritually in tune, we become the witness who is aware of what was said but we don't get stuck in it. We know the truth behind all of the effects of life. The purpose of spiritual practices is not to get things done fast, but to give us the ability to maintain awareness at all times.

There are three basic spiritual practices. The first one is spiritual mind treatment, which we use to address the emotional and physical concerns of life. The second is meditation, which is more absolute. It helps us realize we are more than our circumstances and our body. We are a spiritual being on an infinite journey of unfoldment. Meditation gives us perspective and expands our consciousness so we see things in the whole instead of tiny parts. The third practice is selfless service to God, which is called

Seva in Sanskrit language. Seva supports our idea of wholeness and can go with us everywhere, no matter what we are doing. Seva is an attitude of doing our regular daily routine for God's sake and for our own spiritual progress.

Seva can be used as a spiritual practice when fixing dinner. For instance, we might be making chicken, carrots, and rice. In an ordinary sense we look at this food as just chicken, carrots, and rice. With the attitude of Seva, we look at each piece of food as one form that God has taken. It is a miracle—God is in my kitchen in the form of a carrot! It is just one example of God doing what God does perfectly—create! When we cut the carrots we do it with love. When we clean and cook the chicken, it is done with love. Now dinner is not ordinary, it is extraordinary.

A Practitioner works in the field of caring by assisting others in seeing truth. We have a natural response to help, to reach out when we see a problem. But sometimes we might draw a line beyond which we won't help. We may feel like we have closed down our heart and are separated from God. In doing service, there are many opportunities where temptation gets us lost in outer circumstances and we forget about the inner truth. Seva brings us back. When we are spiritually undernourished, Seva is one of the greatest ways to get food for the soul. New energy shows up and we see every moment of life as supremely blessed regardless of circumstances.

If we are working with someone who is very sick, our gift of Seva is to let go of any barriers or feelings of separateness and just be together, meeting the person on a plane of unity, love, and compassion. If mind gets caught up in sympathy or pity, a wall is created where we identify more as a helper and force the other person into the role of one being helped. Seva helps the Practitioner resolve any fear and discomfort about a client so they can assist the client in the revelation of truth. There is no one being helped. There are only two beings relating together in unity and love.

There are so many opportunities for Seva and one way is using a witness consciousness. Let our reactions to any situation fall away. Open our hearts and see God in it all. Seva is an attitude and a decision, recognizing God creates through everything. Everything serves everything, at work, at home, and at play. When we go to work and recognize it as an experience of God, we can actually feel the difference and experience the goodness of life.

Instead of feeling unhappy and anxious about anything, we use spiritual practices to fine tune our mind which helps us to see through temporary appearances. In the same way we need air, water, and food, in the spiritual world we need nourishment. Seva is one way to find God in all. At that point every moment of life is supremely blessed regardless of circumstances.

Chapter 22

Relationship To 12-Step Programs

Twelve-step recovery programs continue to be a very popular and successful way to address addictive behavior problems. Practitioners may be contacted by someone enrolled in one of many twelve-step programs available in most communities. Typically the person is not requesting the work of a Practitioner or a client session, but instead will ask the Practitioner to be a nonjudgmental listener as they work through one of the steps. Some of the characteristics of addictive behavior include grandiosity, judgmentalism, intolerance, impulsivity, indecisiveness, dishonesty, controlling, or self-centeredness. In order to better understand the process of twelve-step programs, a discussion of the steps may be helpful.

SURRENDER STEPS: Acknowledge the problem

1) Admitting they are powerless over the addiction and their life has become unmanageable. Only a person being healed will be able to say this; a person in denial will not. Admitting they are powerless frees them from self-delusion. It stops the instinctual reaction to control something that was out of control. Insanity would be doing

the same thing and expecting the results to be different. This step confronts denial, which often shows up as blaming, despair, or various control issues. A Practitioner may see this step as coming to grips with reality, the situation here and now, the effect.

2) Recognizing that there is a power greater than they are that can restore sanity. This hands the problem over to God. A Practitioner may recognize this as knowing I, an individual, am not the doer.
3) Deciding to turn over willpower and their life to the care of a Higher Power. This requires taking action and letting go of control without knowing the results. It begins a personal relationship with God.

These first three steps get their bloated nothingness out of the way.

ACTION STEPS:

4) Inventorying their life. The list includes liabilities in three areas: resentments, fears, harm done to themselves and others. It confronts their own character defects and fears, showing how they not only create their own pain but perpetuate it. Through this, they can then outline an ideal situation and know it can be created.
5) Admitting the nature of their wrongs to the Higher Power and another human being. This helps overcome rationalization or fooling oneself. It is challenging because it lets someone else see who they are and what they have done. This is a powerful step in taking responsibility for their behavior, forgiving themselves and accepting forgiveness.
6) Trusting in a Higher Power, allowing a new start in life to begin.
7) Asking the Higher Power to remove any shortcomings. This includes doing an inventory of their liabilities or excesses, asking God to remove the blocks that shut out the light of Spirit. It is an exercise in self-honesty. Anyone studying Science of Mind may find

it easy to stay in denial by refusing to look at a condition. Since anyone in addiction despises themselves and feels very disconnected with their feelings, this step helps get reconnected.

8) Inventorying all they have harmed in their life and be willing to make amends. This action step recognizes they are no longer helpless.
9) Making amends whenever possible, except when doing so would injure oneself or others. This sets up the ability to go into recovery. The Practitioner knows that what one thinks they were in the past can continue to impact the present. Making amends can heal the past and make running away unnecessary. It shows a willingness to heal their attitude and take personal responsibility. Three lists of amends are required: l) people they can make amends to now, 2) people they can make amends to later, and 3) people they will never make amends to. Usually by the time they are half way through list #2, list #3 doesn't look so impossible.

MAINTENANCE STEPS:

10) Admitting when they are wrong by continuing to take a personal inventory. It becomes a daily habit that helps build a consciousness that supports their good and gets rid of "stinking thinking". It creates a change in behavior in a solution-oriented way.
11) Meditating and praying to improve their contact with the Higher Power, asking for knowledge of Its will and the personal power to carry it out. This has a calming effect and helps decrease the stress level, allowing the person a more objective evaluation of their actions.
12) Practicing principles in all areas of their life. They are now powerful enough to begin helping others.

These steps are not in conflict with Science of Mind. Treatment and applying Science of Mind principles is not an easier, softer way. Spiritual awakening and overcoming an addiction are both processes. In both cases there is no magic fix. Treatment and 12-steps begin with addressing Cause. Like any fix, it starts at the beginning.

Relationship To 12-Step Programs

QUESTIONS FOR DISCUSSION

1. Explain the Science of Mind principle: We are surrounded by this Creative Mind, which receives the direct impress of our thought and acts upon it.
2. When would a Practitioner recommend a 12-step program to a client?
3. How would a Practitioner assist or support someone in a 12-step program?

RECOMMENDED READING

The Edinburgh & Dore Lectures on Mental Science, pages 167-182
The Science of Mind, pages 553-567
Your Mind Can Heal You, pages 182-200

Chapter 23

Thoughts On The Nature Of Immortality

By Dr. James Golden

Many people are curious about what happens when we die. Personally I think death is highly overrated. I think we will be in the same place then as we are now—not in structure, but in consciousness. We take ourselves with us wherever we go.

Death is often seen as something that occurs in the future after which we will be in this great place doing great things. But what about the past, before this lifetime? The last time we died this is where we came. The reason it seems so strange is too often we keep spiritual things in one place and material things in another. When it is time to leave our physical body then we'll be with all that spiritual stuff; God will be there, maybe Aunt Martha, but then again so might Uncle Frank.

Religious Science points out that what we call Spirit and matter are actually the same thing appearing in different guises. God is all of this, not behind it or off to the right or left side. Spirit and matter are the same, so dying is no big deal; the universe will not change a bit. In fact it is our relationship to the Universe that changes and opens up a new level of experience. We no longer have a physical body, but since God is all that is, whatever is true now will be true then. The rules don't change. Therefore, death will not solve our problems.

Death should not be seen as a way of resolving conflict. If we are sick or in a bad relationship, death is not a way out. Our consciousness goes with us wherever we go. When people choose suicide as a solution, the problems they could not cope with in this life go with them into the next dimension. Sooner or later we have to solve our problems. Wonderful opportunities exist to resolve any issue while we are here. In one way or another all of the great spiritual teachers say we are as spiritual now in a physical body as we're going to get. We don't become more spiritual when we die. Our body wouldn't exist unless we were a spiritual being. I've never seen a body without a spiritual being inside of it. The point is, don't build your hopes or expectations into tomorrow. Realize God has given us the authority and power to live life the way we see fit now. We don't have to die to get better. Death is not the place where we get to do whatever we want, actually this life is—this life is heaven. We are doing what we want every minute, given all of our considerations, opinions, and beliefs. Here and now is the time to do what we want. Don't wait for other people, a pay raise, a healthy body, etc., to do what you want. Today is the appointed time.

In many spiritual teachings, death seems very scary because it is described as a place where we lose control. When we watch people die, some go peacefully and others struggle in anguish and worry. Death is the final test of this life so don't wait and cram for the exam in the last few days. If we live well then we will die well. It isn't being dead that is hard, it is letting go of the physical body. The same challenges we have living are the same challenges we will have dying. If we are a martyr today and don't change, we'll be a martyr at death. If we see death as a failure, it will be tremendous struggle. We should not wait until the moment before death to cram in happiness and love, but instead work to bring ourselves to the point where we feel complete and happy. Then we can easily release and let go.

We have an unknown amount of time left on this plane so there are no excuses for not resolving difficulties and living fully. No whining there is not enough time, money, training, no one understands or society is flawed. The reason we use excuses for living is we don't have enough courage to feel, accept, or appreciate what we have. Holding back in life is fear and the antidote to fear is courage; courage is the answer. To do what we want to do, start by acknowledging the self. Terry Cole-Whitaker coined a very powerful phrase. "What other people think of you is none of your business." We know in Religious Science that what we think of ourselves is what we become. It takes great spiritual courage to think well of ourselves.

Immortality is a present experience, not something that comes later. It is a state of mind; we already are a spiritual being that always will be. There is no promise that after death our experiences will get better. What we are looking for is an understanding that will allow us to get on with life now. So when we contemplate what to do, listen for excuses that are in the way, and have the courage to get rid of them; they are not true. Let excuses die so we can be fully alive. We are immortal spiritual beings with the full power of God at our disposal. It doesn't get any better than this. God is like a puppy dog that wants to romp and play. We can push the puppy away by thinking our problems are too overwhelming, or we can courageously overcome problems so we can play the game of life. We are what we think we are. We couldn't have any more freedom than we do right now. We are a spiritual being in a universe that says it is done unto us as we believe.

There is only one rule in the universe and that is we make the rules. That is ultimate freedom. It is not an afterlife experience. Our physical body is not in the way, our negative ideas are in the way. Death opens many doors and allows us to see the universe from a different perspective.

Let's not wait until death to become our true self, it would be very disappointing. Say "I love you" now to family and friends and then look inside and let that greatness shine. Realize there is an answer to every challenge, every dilemma. This is immortality.

Chapter 24

The Practitioner Log Book

The Practitioner Log Book is a reminder of the importance of daily spiritual practices and is an ongoing record of your work. As an intern, you will be required to maintain a log for periodic review by your minister. As a Licensed Practitioner, the log records your ongoing dedication to service and personal growth and is reviewed by your minister annually. The following are examples of the various forms (which can be enlarged on a copier) you might consider, or be creative and design your own.

Another important form is the RSI Demonstration Form, which must be used as provided by RSI. It is to be completed by the client when their demonstration occurs. A minimum of five cases are submitted to your minister, who chooses the top three that will be submitted to RSI with your license application. These will be the strongest and best demonstrations of your work.

Practitioner Log Book Sheets

Daily Spiritual Practices
Sunday Attendance And Service
Reading And Tapes
Classes And Workshops
Client Report
Practitioner Receipts

DAILY SPIRITUAL PRACTICES
FOR THE MONTH OF __________

DAY	MEDITATION	JOURNALING	READING	TREATMENT
1	________	________	________	________
2	________	________	________	________
3	________	________	________	________
4	________	________	________	________
5	________	________	________	________
6	________	________	________	________
7	________	________	________	________
8	________	________	________	________
9	________	________	________	________
10	________	________	________	________
11	________	________	________	________
12	________	________	________	________
13	________	________	________	________
14	________	________	________	________
15	________	________	________	________
16	________	________	________	________
17	________	________	________	________
18	________	________	________	________
19	________	________	________	________
20	________	________	________	________
21	________	________	________	________
22	________	________	________	________
23	________	________	________	________
24	________	________	________	________
25	________	________	________	________
26	________	________	________	________
27	________	________	________	________
28	________	________	________	________
29	________	________	________	________
30	________	________	________	________
31	________	________	________	________

SUNDAY SERVICE AND HOW I WAS IN SERVICE

DATE	ATTENDED	SERVICES	PERFORMED	OTHER
1				
2				
3				
4				
5				
6				
7				
8				
9				
10				
11				
12				
13				
14				
15				
16				
17				
18				
19				
20				
21				
22				
23				
24				
25				
26				
27				
28				
29				
30				
31				

READING AND TAPES

MONTH/YEAR	BOOK	AUTHOR

CLASSES AND WORKSHOPS

DATE	TITLE AND INSTRUCTOR	LOCATION	HOURS

CLIENT REPORT

CLIENT________________________________ DATE __________

ADDRESS____

PHONE____

CASE

____

____

BACKGROUND

MENTAL CAUSE

TREATMENT FOCUS

RESULTS

PRACTITIONER RECEIPTS FOR THE YEAR ______

DATE	CLIENT	AMOUNT	CHECK NO.

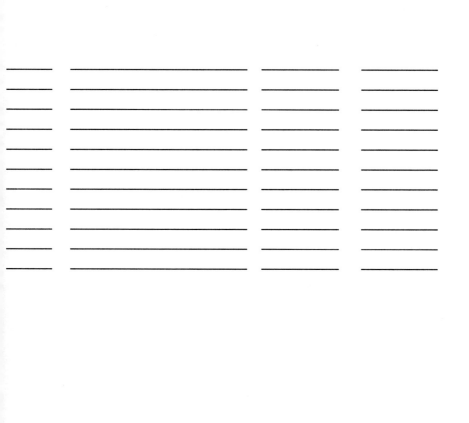

Chapter 25

Thoughts On Spiritual Practices

By Dr. James Golden

Spiritual practices dive deeply into the subconscious to bring out the basis of our life. We know our history but not necessarily why we did or didn't do something. For more understanding, we must look for underlying motives or beliefs. Why are we resentful of others in our life? Why do we have the experience of being a martyr?

There are two reasons to do spiritual practices. One is to understand we are the authors of our experience, life is a reflection of our mind, and the physical universe is a mirror of our consciousness. As God creates in the macrocosm, we create in the microcosm of our individual experience. For most of us this is an unconscious process, but through spiritual practices the direct connection is revealed.

The second reason we do spiritual practices is to implement change. Once we understand our beliefs, we change what needs to be changed. The spiritual truth is God dwells within us as us and the spiritual path enables us to find that essence. Having God as a first hand experience is best. Since we are all unique, we are bound to have different personal experiences of God. At the birth of a baby, weddings or christenings, it is typical to experience tremendous joy and happiness. This is a direct experience of God. We've all tasted it and would like to be in that place more often. This is the goal: to live in a sense of oneness with the Universe, oneness with God. The purpose of spiritual practices is to let the nature of God within reveal itself.

Think about the sun and the moon. When we look at the moon we might think it is giving off light, but the moon's light comes from the sun. Moonlight is sunlight bouncing off the moon. The ego is like the moon with none of its own light. The real source of light is God, the sun. The goal of spiritual practices is not to get the sun to shine brighter, it is to polish the moon so that the light of the sun reflects perfectly. Spiritual practices polish the moon in us by filling in the valleys and honing down the mountains. In this way we receive the light and reflect the amount of God we are attuned to.

One of the benefits of spiritual practices is to focus our wandering mind and its seemingly endless chatter. When we enjoy a sunset, our mind takes in a larger reality and the chatter seems to go away. Notice when we aren't busy doing and thinking so much, God shows up automatically. Spiritual practices increase this sense of spaciousness. If you have ever watched a glass of waterfall over, it may seem to fall in slow motion. At times things seem to take longer. It is an example of heightened consciousness; our mind expands in a given period of time. The more enlightened we are, the more time and space we have for every second of the clock. Objective time stays the same but the experience of self expands vertically. When we say we are one with God, it is not just horizontally but vertically as well.

The earth is part of the solar system, which is part of the Milky Way, which is part of the universe—part of things into infinity. Another goal is to have more subjective time than objective time so we can see what is happening more clearly and appreciate all of life's options. In the East they call this a witness consciousness; the ability to see the unfoldment of our thoughts and beliefs as if they weren't our own. Having more mental time versus physical time creates a calmness and inner peace, which enables us to change patterns of the past that have not yielded positive results. With a witness consciousness we see the lawful benefit of giving and receiving and how to deal with things like anger, so we can perceive the results of anger and choose another path. Witness consciousness enhances our goal of self-discovery so we see our true self.

How strong is the ego? Since ego is our collection of opinions and beliefs, it can be very very strong. If ego represents the truth of our being accurately, it's great, but if it is autonomous and has its own opinions, many mistakes can be made. The dilemma is that even when there are great moments, we find negative thoughts and desires creeping in. Life never seems to be perfect for long. People who walk the spiritual path are happy all of the time. We may or may not ever get to that level, but we can begin the path and use spiritual practices to experience a greater degree of happiness. If there was a magic video that took a snapshot of our mind every second, and every thought was replayed nightly to friends and family, it wouldn't be pleasant. Ego can be that way. What if every thought became manifest instantly? For awhile it would be fun having the Midas touch, but can the ego really be trusted to manifest good thoughts consistently?

In life, we point ourselves in the right direction, realizing we will never attain perfection, and appreciate the benefits. The ego that wants to do spiritual practices in order to be divine can't do it because the motive is selfish. If our intent is to "get" divinity, it won't work. We must give up and surrender in the ego sense. That is when the power of God shows itself. How can a flashlight reveal the sun? By allowing the sun to illumine the flashlight.

Thank goodness only those thoughts and beliefs we repeat again and again become manifest. As our consciousness unfolds, the more easily positive thoughts yield positive results. Spiritual practices help purify our mind to create a healthy reality. The deeper issue is self-discovery. In life we know the beginning and the end; our job is to discover the middle. Spiritual practices bring to the surface all of the issues in life that are waiting to be addressed. Then it is our job to face and resolve each one.

Spiritual realization is not linear. We cannot take a series of lessons and expect every lesson will automatically take us further in our knowledge of truth. It is not a step by step process because it is not a logical process. Looking for God with our mind is like looking for the sun with a flashlight. Looking for the greater light with a lesser light doesn't work. Truly what we are looking for we are looking with. Linear thinking says if we meditate for so many minutes each day, we'll get the prize. That is pushing and forcing life. Instead, live for meditation and let everything be subject to it. Give spiritual practices the highest priority because it makes life better and better. As Gandhi said "Full effort is full victory." Greater peace of mind, happiness, and love will be the result.

Chapter 26

Meditation And Religious Science

It is interesting that often we do not feel closest to Spirit at moments of intense activity, but instead, we find a connection deep inside when we are quiet. Meditation is a powerful tool for expanding the quiet moments when we connect with the sacred, sense deep inner peace, the joy of life without effort, and make space for answers to be revealed.

Meditation, like many other spiritual practices throughout the world, has not been a cornerstone of Religious Science. Yet while the practice of meditation may not be detailed in *The Science of Mind*, it is mentioned in the text, along with the power of silence. We can feel the strength of Dr. Holmes opinion about meditation as a tool when he wrote, "And so we meditate daily upon the Universe of the All Good, the Infinite Indwelling Spirit, which we call God, the Father, Incarnate in man, trying to sense and to feel this Indwelling Good as the Active Principle of our lives…for there is what we seem to be, and what we really are…and as we daily meditate upon this Indwelling God, we shall acquire a greater mental equivalent." By using both meditation and spiritual mind treatment, Holmes was confident, "The one who wishes scientifically to work out his problems, must daily take the time to meditate and mentally treat the condition, no matter what the apparent contradictions may be. He is working silently in the Law and the Law will find an outlet through his faith in It." Silence, meditation and treatment are a powerful combination.

> *We comprehend the Infinite only to the degree that It expresses itself through us, becoming to us that which we believe It to be. So we daily practice in our meditations the realization of Life.*
>
> *Ernest Holmes*

How do we know meditation will be powerful for us? We do not know unless we try it. So how do we begin? Although there is no one right or wrong way to meditate, there are an array of ideas and processes taught around the world that can be used as guidelines. What did Holmes advise? He wrote, "It is through the teachings of the illumined that the Spiritual Universe reveals Itself, imparting to us what we know about God. What we directly experience ourselves, and what we believe others have experienced, is all we can know about God." This is how Holmes learned, by studying the teachings of great spiritual leaders throughout history, the mystics, the illumined. He felt the mystics were great revealers of the nature of the Universe and our relationship to God. We can learn the basics of meditation by studying their knowledge, their wisdom and methods of connecting with the sacred.

Holmes found it fascinating that light comes with an expansion of consciousness. "The light shines in the darkness and the darkness comprehend it not." John 1:5. This pathway of light that is created through the expansion of consciousness, whether it is through spiritual mind treatment or meditation, is not something we create; it is something that pre-exists and we tap into it. All of the great mystics understood this and the more frequently we tap into it, the greater clarity we will achieve.

Some of the easier-to-understand teachings about meditation come from eastern mystics. One such mystic, Paramahansa Yogananda, defined meditation is his book, *Journey To Self-Realization*, "The concentration upon God. The term is used in a general sense to denote practice of any technique for interiorizing the attention and focusing it on some aspect of God. In the specific sense, meditation refers to the end result of successful practice of such techniques: direct experience of God through intuitive perception. It is the 7th step of the eightfold path of Yoga described by Patanjasli, achieved only after one has attained that fixed concentration within whereby he is completely undisturbed by sensory impressions from the outer world. In deepest meditation one experiences the 8th step of the Yoga path: communion, oneness with God."

> *Superior intelligence was not given to the human being merely to be used to eat breakfast, lunch, and dinner; marry and beget children. It was given that man might understand the meaning of life and find soul freedom.*
>
> *Paramahansa Yogananda*

In *The Heart of the Buddha*, Chogyam Trungpa describes meditating as developing mindfulness, which he feels should not be regarded as a minority-group activity or some specialized, eccentric pursuit. "It is a worldwide approach that relates to all experience: it is tuning in to life." This is emphasized in the philosophy of Thich Nhat Hanh, a Vietnamese Zen Master who currently teaches the Four Foundations of Mindfulness at his Plum Village retreat center in France. Here practitioners develop the art of meditating on the mind to be able to see the interdependence of the subject of knowledge and the object of knowledge. He explains that to calm our thoughts we must practice mindfulness of our feelings and perceptions, to know how to observe and recognize the presence of every feeling and thought arising in us. He feels that to receive the full benefits of meditation, we first must build up our power of concentration through the practice of mindfulness in everyday life. Holmes studied the teachings of Buddha, one of the most well-known teachers of meditation and wrote about him in his book, *The Voice Celestial*:

> *Man cannot change the law but he can change*
> *The sequences. The Noble Eightfold Path*
> *Will lead to his emancipation, for*
> *He who fills the stream of consciousness*
> *With Noble Truths and Love shall cause its depth*
>
> *Of waters to run clear: he shall be held*
> *From pains of guilt, which dying out will set*
> *Him free to enter in Nirvana.*

The Buddha realized the benefit of meditation when he discovered that struggling to find answers did not work. Described by Chogyam Trungpa in, *Cutting Through Spiritual Materialism*, "It was only when there were gaps in his struggle that insights came to him. He began to realize that there was a sane, awake quality within him which manifested itself only in the absence of struggle. So the practice of meditation involves "letting be," trying to go with the pattern, trying to go with the energy and the speed."

In the Siddya Yoga tradition, Swami Muktananda explained that one-pointed concentration is used by all of us at one time or another, such as when we take a test, cook food, or garden. Using this same ability to concentrate our focus on our love for God is meditation, a mind free from thoughts. Another teacher describes it as expanding the space between our thoughts. Through this process we find the place of supreme peace within.

If you meditate on your ideal, you will acquire its nature. If you think of God day and night, you will acquire the nature of God.

Sru Ramakrishna

Holmes found Jesus' description of going into the silence very insightful and wrote: "He (Jesus) told us that in prayer we should enter the closet and close the door… Entering the closet means withdrawing into one's own mind. For it is from one's own mind that the creativeness which one possesses emanates." Through the ages this 'closet' has been described at various times as the Secret Place of the Most High, the Tabernacle of the Almighty, the Holy of Holies, the place to *Be Still And Know I Am God.*

The term meditation, as used by Catholic mystics, often refers to a form of prayer where one ponders Christ and, as Carol Lee Finders describes in her book, *Enduring Grace,* "See (the Passion of Christ) as vividly as possible to the mind's eye, moving about from one element to another. The more intensely focused kind of mental activity that constitutes meditation for many of us today is closer to what Catholic mystics would have regarded as mental prayer or interior prayer, which becomes in its most advanced stages, contemplative prayer."

Author's Nick Bakalar & Richard Balkin explain in *The Wisdom of John Paul II,* that although in the Christian tradition there are several definitions of prayer, it is most often described as a talk, a conversation with God. "Conversing with someone, not only do we speak but we also listen. Prayer, therefore, is also listening. It consists of listening to hear the interior voice of grace. Listening to hear the call. And then you ask me how the Pope prays, I answer you: like every Christian—he speaks and he listens. Sometimes, he prays without words, and then he listens all the more. The most important thing is precisely what he 'hears.'"

Although types and styles of meditation vary around the world, any practice of meditation can bring us to that perfect state of awareness over time, where we are just one with everything; we observe without judgment; we sit is smiling repose. Meditation also unleashes in us a tremendous level of peace, love, and compassion. Who wouldn't want more of this in their life! But although meditation seems simple, it can be very challenging at the same time, because we grow as our ability to meditate grows.

When we begin meditating what tends to come to the forefront of our thoughts is what is described as "the basic neurosis of mind," which is the relationship between ourselves and our world. As we meditate we begin to understand our thought pattern as well. We can see thoughts as just that…thoughts. If we judge our thoughts obsessively, whether condemning or praising, we actually feed and encourage them.

Chogyam Trungpa describes this process in *The Myth Of Freedom.* "A person always finds when he begins to practice meditation that all sorts of problems are brought out. Any hidden aspects of your personality are brought out into the open, for the simple reason that for the first time you are allowing yourself to see your state of mind as it is.

> *The teaching of the mystics has been that there should be conscious courting of the Divine Presence. There should be a conscious receptivity to It, but a balanced one.*
>
> *Ernest Holmes*

For the first time you are not evaluating your thoughts." Dealing with these thoughts is all part of the process of achieving inner peace. Ram Dass feels it is important to have some understanding what the game of life is about to want to meditate. This popular American meditation teacher explains the challenge in his book, *Grist For The Mill.* "So we have a little bit of wisdom, and then we try to concentrate. But every time we try to concentrate, all of our other desires, all of our other connections and clingings to the world keep pulling on us all the time. So we have to clean up our game a little bit; that is purification, and then our meditation becomes a little deeper. As our meditation gets deeper we are quieter and we are able to see more of the universe so that wisdom gets deeper and we understand more. The deeper wisdom makes it easier to let go of some of the attachments, which makes it easier to increase right livelihood. All three things keep interweaving with one another; they are a beautiful balancing act." Some people experience the fear of emptiness or nothingness as the mind releases thoughts and there is a moment when we are not relating to someone or something. Although the fear is not real, that sense of floating without a personal identity causes us to hold back. But as the practice continues, we begin to trust the process and ourselves even more.

Many people try meditation to relieve pain, anxiety, tension or sadness. Yet what often comes to mind in the early stages of meditation is the recognition of how protective we are of certain people, places, or things or the particular way we experience life. Every time we recognize another level of attachment in life, we find our growing edge…the next area for more inner work. By continuing to pursue spiritual growth, there will be some point where we suddenly find the hardest work has been left behind. At this point our lessons are easier and our joy more profound.

Practicing meditation daily until it becomes a habit is the key. As Yogananda so wisely taught, "Habits of yielding to passions result in suffering. Habits of yielding to the mechanical routine of worldly life beget monotony, indifference, vexation, worry, fear, disgust, disillusionment. Habits of attending church and sacred lectures produce fitful inspiration and momentary desire for God. But habits of devotional meditation and concentration produce realization." This is the gift of making meditation a daily habit in our lives.

During the experience of pure consciousness the sense of the here-and-now fades away and one experiences a merger with something greater than the individual self...in which the ego and the sense of individual self are transcended.

Larry Dossey

When we recognize our Spirit is experiencing life through our body for a purpose, we can find out more about our soul's wants, needs and desires through the practice of meditation. Since Spirit is larger than the confines of our body, it is valuable to get more attuned with it, so that we can see and understand life from a position greater than what we observe by just being a human being. Our subconscious mind experiences unity with all, contains all knowledge and is the avenue through which we connect with the Divine. We can access this vast library of information and bring it into our conscious mind through meditation, and at the same time increase our ability to let intuitive thought surface more easily and clearly to guide us on a daily basis.

Throughout the ages the mystics have taught the value of consciously courting the Divine. Holmes taught that illumination comes as we more frequently realize our Unity with the Whole, and constantly endeavor to let the Truth operate through us. But since we connect with the Whole at the point of our subconscious, it will be here alone that we will contact It. He cautioned that perceiving the Self is somewhat like entering a dark room on a bright and sunny day. It takes awhile for our eyes to adjust. It takes awhile for us mentally to adjust to meditation so that we may experience what lies beyond this physical body and our mind.

To assist us in the process, it is helpful to use rituals. Not that a ritual represents any religious belief, but rituals are effective ways to help focus our mind on the inner self. Should you feel any resistance to these suggestions, ignore them, but do not let it stop you from doing basic meditation practices. The most important ritual or step in the process is to find a quiet place to sit where we are not distracted or interrupted. It can be as simple as the corner of a bedroom or study, or in walking meditation using a quiet park, back yard or garden. In sitting meditation, the body position should be comfortable to discourage fidgeting or a desire to sleep. Traditionally this is a cross-legged sitting position with hands in the lap, but you can sit comfortably in a chair or against a wall. The back is held naturally straight without tension, shoulders back. After taking this position several times, our body and mind quickly begin to settle down when we assume "the position" since subconsciously we have accepted this as the beginning of meditation.

> *There is no greater obstacle to union*
> *with God than time.*
>
> *Meister Eckhart*

Through rituals the mind will soon begin quieting down as we prepare for meditation. This can be triggered by simply meditating in the same place each day, then as we approach the "place," our mind recognizes it is time to meditate. Having items around us that are symbolic of our Oneness also trigger this calming effect. It can be anything that reminds us of our true nature, such as a candle. Perhaps a rock or shell from a special place, or picture of a loved one or spiritual teacher will help our mind to settle down. Creating the atmosphere for meditation can include wearing the same clothing, blanket or shawl for warmth. Each time we put on that clothing, the mind will begin to quiet down.

The goal of preparing to meditate is to create a mind free of all thought, yet be fully aware. We let go of memories. We stop creating or solving problems, or dreaming about the future. Our goal is a mind that focuses on the present, not the past or the future. Meditation is the process of reaching the recognition of the eternal present moment. The good news: it is a process that improves with practice. In the early stages, it is natural to watch the mind become hyperactive at the same time we wish it would calm down. Or the mind finally quiets down and just then a thought comes rushing in, we follow it, and the quietness is gone. Noises or bodily functions can distract us. Many things can take us away from the silence, so it is important to recognize meditation as a process that improves over time.

Various methods can be used to pursue the silence. One of the most traditional is following the breath, focusing on each in-breath and each out-breath. This one-point focus helps us reach that place called the "witness consciousness," where we are just consciously aware of our body functions. This helps us to be the observer when thoughts arise, but we do not feel a need to cling to them. We just let them go away. Another method to still the mind is the repetition of one or more words or sounds. In yoga this is called a mantra. Repeating the words "I AM" or a phrase like, "God Is Love," can still the mind and open the heart. Chanting is even a more powerful way to open the heart and tap into oneness. Chanting with a tape in a "call and response" fashion, can release tension and build our energy level. There ere are many chanting and meditation tapes and CD's on the market today. Some are more traditional and a very comfortable beginning for those who want to try chanting as a pathway to deep meditation. The chant can be as simple as repetition of the words "Alleluhia," "Kyrie" and "Om Namah Shivaya." Sometimes just listening to a Native American pan flute helps me reach that place.

The length of meditation depends on the one meditating. Ideally, begin with five minutes and gradually increase it to 30 minutes a day. If you have the opportunity to meditate one hour or more with a group, it can be a life-changing experience, but for a typical daily practice, 30-minutes is very beneficial.

We are trying to get peace or happiness from outside, from money or power. But real peace, tranquility, should come from within.

The Dalai Lama

Signs of progress in meditation include an increasing sense of peacefulness; a conscious inner experience of calmness that expands into bliss; finding answers to questions through the intuitive state; increasing mental and physical efficiency; the desire to hold on to the peace and joy of the meditative state; expanding unconditional love towards our loved ones; actual contact with God, with that which is beyond all creation.

Holmes cautioned us not to just meditate for meditation's sake, because he felt "a passive meditation will never produce an active demonstration, any more than an artist can paint a picture by sitting down with his paints but never using them." He felt we should read, study, think and meditate upon statements that calm us, give us poise and confidence, while erasing all thoughts of fear and tension. The Dalai Lama cautions, "It is easier to meditate than to actually do something for others. But to merely meditate on compassion is to take the passive option. Our meditation should form the basis for action, for seizing the opportunity to do something. The motivation of the meditator and sense of universal responsibility should be expressed in deeds."

The result of any spiritual practice is we are called to action. Bless your life and the life of others, your community, and the world by using meditation as a powerful tool for growth and understanding.

There is only one Power and one Presence in the Universe. It exists in, as and through everything, so all of creation operates in absolute harmony and balance. Its expressions are limitless, and my experience forever reveals this. My true nature expresses Spirit through every aspect of my being, and I move courageously into ever-expanding circles of joy.

Chapter 27

Ernest Holmes On Practitioners

THE ETHICS OF OUR PROFESSION

(Stenographic report of lecture on Friday, May 5, 1933)

Whether or not a great many of us ever expect to be professional practitioners is entirely outside of the question. We should all practice, either for ourselves or for someone else. Many will become professional practitioners and will be successful or not according to their own states of consciousness. Here is the only thing in the world that I know of, everything depends upon our state of consciousness.

To begin with, a Practitioner establishes themself in practice not because they work from an institution which has a great background, but because they know how to practice, and practices. There isn't any other way they can ever be permanently or successfully established. If they do this, there is nothing that can keep them from becoming established. It has nothing to do with personality; it is entirely within their own mind and never with anything else. And so if people say to me, "How shall I get established in practice?" I say, "Begin to practice in your own mind and it will not be long before you will have clients." Then they ask, "How are people to know about it?" I do not know how they know about it. How do we know we are alive? There isn't anyone living who can tell us by what power we are able to stand up and speak. Science watches the process of that being and neither science, religion, nor philosophy can explain, but has to accept on faith.

Do not feel that you have to know it all. The person who thinks they know it all is a very fortunate individual. If there could be anyone who knew it all, what a terrific position the Universe would be in. It would mean that God would be exhausted or Cosmic Life would die of boredom. There isn't any system of thought or any person who can know it all. Such an attitude stamps a person as being intellectually stupid. The Practitioner, then, isn't one who pretends to know it all. They isn't anyone who thinks that all they have to do is wave their wand. That is not the approach we make to this thing. In fact, that is the attitude that makes this movement queer in the eyes of intelligent people, and we wish to avoid it for the sake of the movement and the good it will do.

The thing we believe in is the most intensely intelligent of any philosophy the world has ever conceived because it is the effect of getting together all the best the world has ever known. The Practitioner is one who is trying in their own mind to see that we are living in a spiritual Universe, disregarding the material evidence which contradicts that assumption; that the spiritual Universe is in harmony; that it is a Unity and is perfect. We know that it does not seem to be so. We know that wherever we look this thought is contradicted by appearance, and we know that appearance and reality are, or may be, entirely different things. Consequently, the Practitioner has a principle to demonstrate and that principle is the harmony of the Universe, the unity of all good, the presence and susceptibility of a dynamic power and consciousness and creativeness which we call the Spirit, ever available and ever present. The Practitioner is one who, in the midst of confusion is trying to sense peace and must begin to treat themself for this condition, as we have discussed over and over again.

As a person who understands these things begins to treat mentally and to know that they are able to help people and that such will be drawn to them, they will find that people begin to come to them for help. That is the way they demonstrate a practice. Therefore, they prove for themself that which they will be able to prove for the other person.

There are certain things that we should know about practice. A mental practitioner of any kind should never put their hands on the client. They can be arrested and sent to jail for doing so. They should never prescribe so much as a certain brand of cold cream. Even casual recommendations that we might make to each other outside of practice, we could be arrested for if we were to say the same thing in the profession. The medical profession is very powerful, very critical, and very jealous of its position and it is well in this case that it should be so, for we do not know anything about prescribing remedies. We are not to lay our hands on our clients or to prescribe any kind of medicine. We are to keep our work in its own field, for that is where it belongs and we should never be disturbed by any other field of action. We should never feel disturbed if the client should go to a physician because it will not in any way interfere with our work. Our work is entirely in the field of mind and we must keep it there. Practice, as we understand it, is a combination of straight mental science and a spiritual atmosphere, and both are necessary. A Practitioner knows exactly what they are doing and why they do it from the standpoint of mental science. They bring as much of the spiritual atmosphere to bear on this understanding as they can conceive.

A Practitioner never talks about their clients. If there is any reason for them to take up the discussion of a client from the standpoint of diagnosis, they do it professionally. Never talk about clients to other clients—that is a very great breach of professional conduct; it is not a good thing to do. Such a Practitioner is not likely to be successful. No one knows whom a Practitioner is treating or why. There are certain ethics about this work, which we must be very careful to observe. There is no one who gets closer to people than a Practitioner. Clients tell the innermost secrets of their lives and it is not only very unethical but also very wrong for a Practitioner to run about and destroy or profane this sacred confidence that has been given them.

A Practitioner is not a pious, narrow-minded person, spiritually and intellectually puffed up. A person who has had the greatest experience in life, theoretically should be the best Practitioner. A Practitioner is one who, when people come to them, views them neither as saints nor sinners, but just as people. Whatever their reaction to life may be, whatever their habits of living, the Practitioner does not separate them. They view them only as people and cases, but have no opinion about the cases whatever. If they have, the thing they are going to do is subject to that opinion. Why? Because the thing they do takes place in thought and if they have a preconceived thought or opinion about the client, the efficacy of their treatment will be limited to that opinion. Consequently, the Practitioner views people not as good or bad, but just as people, and the condition as a case, which has to be met. There is no class of people who should be so tolerant and broad-minded and understanding of human reactions. Hence, the Practitioner should not discuss with other people the confidences of their clients—it is a dishonest, unholy thing to do. This confidence is a sacred thing and should never go further than the ears of the Practitioner to whom it should not be considered as anything but the evidence of a certain action and reaction.

A Practitioner must never take a personal responsibility for their client. This is a very subtle thing because in order to do our best work, we have to be sympathetic and kindly disposed and yet at the same time we must be very careful not to mentally enter into the state of consciousness, which gives rise to this condition.

There is another very subtle thing about this practice, which is this: If a person goes into it just with the idea of making money, they are not likely to receive it, but if they practice rightly they will get money. In other words, the

Practitioner's whole attention is to be centered on the concept of their client or the condition as being in an eternal state in Spirit and manifest in Mind, and if they are going to get results. Where our consciousness is centered, our thought and emotions are centered. Our conviction is the affirmative state of our thought and I have noticed in this field above any other (because this field deals entirely with consciousness) that once we have reduced it to a state of thought, then what is going to happen depends on the state of thought. And if a Practitioner's whole reaction is "It is a pretty good thing for me to help this person because of who they are," they had better not try to treat that person. One cannot buy and sell this thing, and one who has the belief that they can is not going to get anywhere by having that state of mind. If a Practitioner, when they come to practice, takes a case for nothing, they must give it just as much time, attention and thought as if they were being well paid.

There are very few walks in life where a person can become such an unconscious liar as they can in this field. Most of our friends will say, "Now you can treat me." They don't know or care whether or not we are doing it and we find that within a week we might have fifty people half-believing they are being treated. We would find ourselves swamped. The very first thing we should say to a friend who approaches us and asks for treatment is, "Are you serious? Do you believe in this thing? Do you understand it? Do you accept it? What is your reaction to it?" Explain to people when they do not understand by saying, "Do you wish me to treat you? Do you realize it will take from fifteen minutes to one hour of my time daily?" It is only fair to people that they should understand this; otherwise the Practitioner will make so many loose promises among their friends, that they will become an unconscious liar. It is very likely that unless friends understand, they will think the Practitioner just bunches everyone together and says a good word for them. The Practitioner may even find themself doing this. Practice is not well-wishing or wishing people well; that is one of the motives back of it, but we have discovered that practice has a definite technique. I wish everyone who studies this thought would realize that unless there were a definite technique it would not be a science. There are certain laws just as real in the mental and spiritual realm, with which we deal, as there are in any other field of action, and we have to deal with them very definitely in the way they work.

The Practitioner should be very specific. Be very frank, open and honest with anyone who comes to you, and make them be very honest with you, because people do have a superstitious reaction and think that a Practitioner just says "God bless all of them." Therefore, a Practitioner, of all people, has to be perfectly straightforward, very honest. They should deal with a case not as a personality gone wrong or exceedingly right, but just as a case undergoing an experience, which is the result of the client personally reacting in a certain way to life. The work is impersonal and the Practitioner can say to their client things that otherwise must seem critical. Be very candid without being critical, and you must be that.

Very few people understand what this practice is; most of the people teaching metaphysics do not understand it. No one's understanding is very great, and many people have hardly any understanding because to most people philosophy is what someone else has taught; religion is what someone else has felt. Too often our religions are our intellectual reactions to other people's concepts rather than our own reactions to an immediate awareness. Therefore, it seems to me that a sincere Practitioner must make up their mind that they are going to spend a great deal of time with themself and if they haven't come to the place in their evolution that they can do that, I do not see how they are going to be a good Practitioner, because the work is entirely within oneself.

A Practitioner must be willing, if necessary, to sit up all night with themself, talking to themself. One is not a good Practitioner unless they are willing to do this. Practice is a sacred thing; reaching the most sacred interior of people's consciousness. Never violate these trusts and remain honest and faithful to a client and oneself. We must be very sure in this practice that our motive is absolutely honest and absolutely right. Practitioners are not well paid for their work, they do not make as much money as they could make by the same amount of work in most any other field. They have to concentrate more than people in most any other profession. Like a physician, they are always on call and unless one is willing to meet these phases of the case, do not go into the field of practice. Fortunately, this field of mental practice is fool-proof—only those people stay in practice who get results, and only those people get results who practice correctly.

We are all in different places in evolution. One man isn't much farther along than another, but one man goes this way while another man goes that way. Let us not let our reaction to this thing be that way. Let us not think there is any person, place, position, influence in life or any opportunism in this work. If our reaction to it in the slightest degree is from the standpoint of opportunism, let us be very honest with ourselves—we don't get anywhere when we do it that way.

Practice is not trying to live another person's life. That is a responsibility we cannot take. Here is what happens: We enter into the state of consciousness, which is theirs and not ours, and that is where we stop. We enter into the reaction, the morbidity, the unhappiness, the fear and the doubt. But that, in itself, would not be so bad if we did not at the same time enter into the belief that we are responsible for their existence. From the highest and the most sincere motive comes that belief, but that can never be. Therefore, the honest-minded Practitioner must be careful not to get caught in this very subtle trap—the belief that we have to be personally responsible for people. We cannot work right for any person unless we can impersonalize the situation. If we find that we cannot, let us try to work for that person. The moment the Practitioner tries to work that way, they enter into the condition they seek to relieve.

Then there is another reaction, which also comes from the highest motive. It is a hang-over from the old theology that we suffer for righteousness' sake. Someday we will stop doing that—I don't know when. Nothing will have happened except that we will stop suffering and gradually learn that lesson as we see that every person, in the long run, will reach best motive, that it is our duty to do everything that everyone wants us to do. It is not our duty any more than it is our duty to go out in the street and lie down and let people scrape their feet on us. Right here we should differentiate between a true and false humility.

If this thing cannot be a thing of spontaneity and joy, it isn't worthwhile. That leads us to human elements. Do not be afraid to be spontaneous; virtue is always unconscious; it is always spontaneous. If we can first come to sense that the human and the Divine are the same thing, that the mind we use in our human reasoning is merely as much of that Mind which we call "Divine" as we are able to use, we shall find that this practice of the spiritual life is the most normal, natural and spontaneous thing. And we will find this, that a lot of people who have never heard of metaphysics are much better metaphysicians than we are; and we will also realize that everywhere we look we are going to learn something.

Don't try to make converts. Don't try to drag all your friends in and make them believe. We need to have the convictions that what we believe is so; we do not need to transmit that conviction to any living soul. If a multitude of men walk down the street and see a granite shaft withstanding the gale, they know it is solid, and if they see a straw blowing in the wind, they know it is just a straw. People are intelligent. In the long run we make an impress on life, which is the exact correspondent of what we actually are.

First, last, and all the time, our whole process is demonstration and that demonstration begins right here. It is the demonstrating of a greater peace in our own life, a greater joy in our own consciousness, a greater spontaneity in our whole expression and a fuller, happier, more successful, and more vital life. People will see things; outside of that we have no mission to convert. Ours is a mission of entering more completely into life for the joy of living. We want that and we shall be a group of people who talk less and do more. Let us practice our belief in our own interior until people see in our daily living the outward result of our inner belief and conviction.

Epilogue

What I Find So Special About Ernest Holmes

By Mary Schroeder

There is no doubt in my mind that Ernest Holmes was a spiritual leader extraordinaire. Raised in New England in the late 1800s, Holmes did not finish high school, yet he had a tremendous enthusiasm for knowledge and truth and thus was an avid reader of books. Over time he was able to piece together the profound knowledge of many of the world's greatest spiritual leaders and thinkers throughout history. He drew from that knowledge a practical application of Law that works to enhance one's connection with Universal Mind and create positive changes and physical healings in daily life.

Like many spiritual leaders, he found joy, financial and personal satisfaction in his work. Holmes loved being a Practitioner and lecturer. He was a unique spiritual leader and teacher, developing classes, writing texts, and giving Sunday lectures to thousands. Many who followed and learned from him wanted more. In this case his followers wanted him to ordain ministers and establish churches, grow the philosophy and lead a growing organization. His greatest concern was that the teachers and churches would uphold the truths and teachings as he discovered them.

The challenge for any spiritual leader is to maintain clarity while helping those who learn and teach the philosophy to become proficient experts. Any teaching that can improve life as much as Religious Science deserves to be available to all of humanity, brought to the attention of the world. This requires many teachers who use a variety of teaching methods, so the leader will find the greatest growth and strength in the organization by focusing on how to help the individual teachers succeed, focus on the results not just the method.

***Holmes gave a 25-word definition of Religious Science*:** **Religious Science is the correlation of laws of science, opinions of philosophy, and revelations of religion applied to human needs and the aspirations of man.** He expected his practitioners and ministers to do daily treatment and depend on God first. In healing others he felt the most important thing is to see the Divinity in everyone. He was proud to say we are a teaching order and a healing order, not a preaching order. One of his messages to Practitioners was to do daily treatment knowing every doorway of opportunity is open to us. Every talent and ability we possess is gladly recognized, welcomed, used and properly compensated for, and to always have a joyous expectancy of success.

Ernest Holmes On Practitioners

QUESTIONS FOR DISCUSSION

1. Explain the Science of Mind principle: We believe in the healing of the sick through the Power of this Mind. We believe in the control of conditions through the Power of this Mind.
2. What is the value of being a Licensed Practitioner with Religious Science International?
3. If Science of Mind is open at the top, will we ever find out we were doing something wrong or in error?
4. How will you know when you are good enough to establish a successful practice as a Practitioner?
5. If a client sees one Practitioner and then goes to another, what does it mean?
6. What if you have your own problems—what should you do?
7. If a client you did Treatment for loses their job or their relationship, what does it mean?
8. Why is it important to do treatment for your church daily?

RECOMMENDED READING

The Edinburgh & Dore Lectures on Mental Science, pages 183-206

Chapter 28

Requisites and Procedures for Licensing

Religious Science International Policy & Procedure book, revised April 1998.

Printed with permission from Religious Science International, 1995.

REQUISITES:

Eligibility for licensing as a Religious Science International Practitioner is determined by the qualifying requisites as follows:

a. Successful completion of SOM I, SOM II and SOM III.
b. Successful completion of the Practitioner Practicum.
c. Application can be made for a First Practitioner License if a student is enrolled in a Practicum class which is scheduled to be completed within 30 days of license approval. Approval is contingent on student's completion of Practicum.

d. Must be affiliated with a Religious Science International Church (this includes retired ministers), and cannot simultaneously hold membership in any other church. A Practitioner license is terminated when membership ceases in the church in which the license was granted, unless said license is transferred to another church.

e. Must be 18 years of age or older.

f. Intern period: The length of time for Practitioner Internship shall be a minimum of one (l) year prior to application, and may be extended at the discretion of the Pastor and/or Intern Field Minister. Exceptions to this policy will be reviewed by the RSI Board of Education's Practitioner Department.

g. Completed SOM III and the Practitioner Practicum, within a maximum of four years or reviewed SOM I, II, III, or IV within three years of application. Note: This ruling also applies to United transfer practitioners not having a current license. Active service in the church warrants special consideration.

PROCEDURE FOR APPLICATION:

1. A first Practitioner application packet includes: Application for (P1), Confidential Information form (I1), three case histories and three completed Verification of Demonstration forms (P3) and an application fee. The necessary forms are available through the RSI Administrative Services.
2. The first Practitioner application fee is: $150.00. Foreign applicants are assessed at the rate of foreign exchange, payable in U.S. currency.
3. The signed recommendation of the applicant's current pastor, through which the application is being submitted, is required. The signed recommendation of the applicants SOM III instructor is also required. If pastorship changes, application will be returned for signature of current Pastor.

Once Pastor reviews completed application and signs, documentation should be mailed to the RSI Administrative Services—Department of Records for verification and distribution to the Chairperson, Department of Practitioner Education and must be received by that office a minimum of thirty (30) days prior to a regularly scheduled RSI Board of Education meeting.

LICENSE RENEWAL:

A Practitioner license must be renewed annually. This will occur prior to the end of each calendar year, with renewal applications sent to the church by the RSI Administrative Services for distribution to the Practitioner.

Upon return receipt and processing of these applications by the RSI Administrative Services, Practitioner licenses will be forwarded to the church for pastors signature and distribution by January l of the year.

To be eligible for Practitioner renewal:

1. Within the three years preceding the request for renewal, the Practitioner must have a minimum of 72 hours of appropriate educational activities and class work selected by the pastor as being consistent with RSI educational standards. Retired ministers are exempt from review classes for Practitioner renewal. Note: The tuition for a Practitioner to review any class is to be determined by the pastor.
2. The Practicum is equivalent to one unit of review credit for Practitioner license renewal.
3. The renewal fee is $100.00 per year, domestic. Foreign renewals are assessed at the rate of foreign exchange, payable in U.S. currency.

Prorate schedule for first renewal following granting of a Practitioner license is as follows:

a. Granted January/February Board meeting:	$100.00
b. Granted April/May Board meeting:	$ 67.00
c. Granted August/September Board meeting:	$ 33.00
If the Fall Board meeting is held in November:	$ 16.00

REINSTATEMENT:

If a Practitioner's license has lapsed over a period of one year, a letter must be submitted to the RSI Administrative Services by the Practitioner's current pastor indicating the desire to reinstate the individuals license, certifying that all educational requirements have been met, and including the required $100.00 renewal fee.

If a Practitioner's license has lapsed three or more years, a review of SOM I, SOM II, or SOM III is required prior to reinstatement.

A Practitioner transferring church membership from one RSI Church to another must have approval of the pastor of the church to which he/she is transferring membership in order to apply for Practitioner reinstatement in the new church.

UNITED PRACTITIONER TRANSFERS:

NOTE: Since United training is not completed until a license is granted by the United Board of Examiners following a personal examination, RSI will only accept Practitioner equivalency with the transfer of an active United Practitioner License.

A current United Practitioner License (within two years) may be transferred to a RSI first Practitioner license upon the recommendation of the pastor of a RSI Church. Information and transfer application packet to include:

a. Practitioner Transfer application form (P2), Confidential Information form (I1), copy of current United Practitioner License, 3 case histories and 3 corresponding Verification of Demonstration forms (P3), and transfer fee. Only United Practitioners complying with the preceding requirements will be recognized as Practitioners in RSI Churches.
b. Transfer and application fee: $225.00 ($150.00 for license, $75.00 for transfer of credits).

If a transferring Practitioner does not hold a current (within two years) Practitioner License, they must have completed SOM III or the Practitioner Practicum, or, have reviewed SOM I, II, III within three years of application.

Note: At the time of acceptance of membership of a church into RSI, all Practitioners of that church will be approved upon request, however, it will require the submission of the required documents. The $150.00 license fee is waived.

A current United minister requesting transfer of their United Practitioner License to an RSIU Practitioner License. Ministers transfer application packet to include:

a. RSI Practitioner First Application (Form P1), copy of current United Practitioner License. Transfer ministers are not required to submit case histories or Verification of Demonstration forms.
b. Transfer and application fee: $225.00 ($150.00 for license, $75.00 for transfer of credits).

MISCELLANEOUS LICENSING INFORMATION:

The Chairperson, Department of Practitioner Education, has the authority to reject a First Practitioner Application.

During the first year of a license, and on the recommendation of the pastor, the RSI Executive Committee has the authority to revoke a Practitioner License.

A Practitioner Certificate will be issued to Practitioners upon approval of a first Practitioner License by the RSI Board of Education's Department of Practitioner Education, and the RSI Board of Directors.

Ordained ministers not currently serving in a ministerial capacity choosing to maintain a current RSI Practitioner License do so through the Office of the President.

PRACTITIONER FEES AS OUTLINED BY THE RSI BOARD:

Single Treatment:	(office or telephone call)	$ 25.00
Home Treatment:	(visit in the home)	$ 50.00
One week treatment:	(office call and daily absent)	$ 75.00
One month treatment:	(daily absent)	$200.00

OUT OF AREA PRACTITIONERS:

Practitioners desiring to be licensed as out-of-vicinity practitioners must receive prior approval from the Board of Education.

United Church of Religious Science Practitioner Code, 1993

Printed with the permission of United Church of Religious Science

ARTICLE II—LICENSING

SECTION 1: LICENSING REQUIREMENTS

A Practitioner's license is granted by the Board of Trustees of the United Church of Religious Science to the candidate who has completed the following requirements for said license:

A. Maintain membership in a member church of the United Church of Religious Science for a minimum of eighteen (18) months immediately prior to application.

B. Be an active, loyal and supporting member of the member church where membership is held. Active means attending church services a majority of the time. Loyal means that a Practitioner shall be an example of one who understands and lives the teachings of the Science of Mind. Supporting includes giving financially to the support of the church in an identifiable manner, such as a check or an offering envelope, and tithing is strongly recommended.

C. The Practitioner of Religious Science may not be, or become, a licensed ordained minister or pastor or practitioner in any other church, denomination, religious faith or spiritual teaching other than the United Church of Religious Science. To do so shall invalidate the Practitioner license. Individuals previously ordained in another denomination, faith, or spiritual organization, but who are no longer active in this ordained capacity must file a letter with the Director of Growth, Education and Ministries testifying that they are inactive and shall not, in any event or manner, apply the powers of the ordination, such as to conduct weddings, church services, etc.

D. Agree to practice faithfully the principles and techniques as taught in The Science of Mind.

E. Agree to abide by the Practitioner Code of Recognition Policy and Procedure and the Church bylaws.

F. Satisfactorily complete all current classwork.

G. Satisfactorily complete the application form provided by the licensing body and pay all required fees.

H. Satisfactorily complete all interviews, written and oral examinations, psychological tests, proficiency standards and other points of qualification as required by the licensing body.

I. In the event the candidate is not passed by the examination panel, reasons and recommendations shall be given. Upon completion of these recommendations as confirmed by the Minister, the candidate may have the right to be re-examined the following year.

SECTION 2: GRANTING OF LICENSE

A. When all requirements for licensing have been met, the candidate's name shall be submitted to the Director of Growth, Education and Ministries to be forwarded to the Board of Trustees for final approval.

B. When the candidate has been approved by the Board of Trustees, a Practitioner license will be issued for a maximum period of two (2) years.

C. The Practitioner Candidate must allow no more than two (2) years to elapse following the completion of required Practitioner course of study prior to initiating the requirements of Article II, Section 1, Item H. Should more than two (2) years elapse the candidate shall be required to audit at least one year (one full course) of the required Practitioner course of study, and should more than five (5) years elapse, the candidates shall be required to retake the entire required Practitioner course of study before initiating the steps required in Article II, Section 1, Items G&H.

SECTION 3: PROFESSIONAL PRACTICE

A. The Licensed Practitioner is entitled to practice the art of Spiritual Mind Treatment professionally in accordance with the principles of The Science of Mind as long as such Practitioner holds a valid Practitioner License.

B. A Practitioner who has met the educational requirements as prescribed and approved by the Board of Trustees, may teach, hold workshops and seminars related to the Science of Mind Principles, under the guidance of the local Minister.

C. A Practitioner may be the director of an authorized study group with the approval of the Director of Growth, Education and Ministries.
D. The Practitioner is not required to maintain his/her practice as the sole source of income; however, aspiring to full time practice is encouraged.

E. The Practitioner shall be available for treatment to the public and shall provide the means by which a client can readily contact him or her.

F. The Practitioner shall establish and charge a fee for service.

G. The Practitioner shall maintain an office and keep appropriate records.

H. Under the Self-Employment Contribution Act of 1943, a Practitioner of Religious Science is legally required to include the income received from services as a Practitioner. A Practitioner should contact the district office of the Director of Internal Revenue Service regarding procedures.

ARTICLE III—RSI PRACTITIONER TRANSFERS

A Practitioner licensed by Religious Science International may be granted a license by the United Church of Religious Science by completing the following requirements:

A. Serve successfully under a provisional license for one year and maintain membership in a member church of United Church of Religious Science during that year.

B. During the provisional year, undertake a personalized course of study, which can include Practitioner I or II, and be supervised by the local Minister.

C. Fulfill requirements B through E of Article II, Section 1.

D. Upon completion of the provisional year, fulfill requirements G and H of Article II, Section 1.

ARTICLE IV—LICENSE RENEWAL

SECTION 1: RENEWAL

A. A Practitioner's license shall remain in force for a period of two (2) years and shall be subject thereafter to biennial renewal.

B. A Renewal Application Form with the current renewal fee must be submitted to the Credentials Coordinator within ninety (90) days following the renewal date. This form is sent to the Practitioner at the time of renewal from the Director of Growth, Education and Ministries. However, it is every Practitioner's responsibility to remain aware of the year during which their license shall lapse and to contact the Division of Growth, Education and Ministries if renewal forms have not reached them by the renewal date. A major purpose of the renewal application form is to ascertain ongoing compliance with the basic requirements for licensing which are maintaining identifiable financial contributions to the local church and remaining an active, loyal and supporting member of that church, as specified in Article VI, Section 4, Item D.

C. First renewal of the license will be contingent upon meeting the basic requirements and upon written documentation of the completion of one hundred (100) hours of service, which may include the following:

1. service clients on a one-to-one basis, but no more than forth (40) hours may be applied in this area;
2. actively participating in a local ministry of prayer;
3. service in a Practitioner role, as directed by the member church Minister.

D. Subsequent license renewal is contingent upon meeting the basic requirements and upon written documentation of the required hours of continuing education as prescribed by both the Standing Advisory

Committee on Practitioner Policy and the Ecclesiastical Officers and as approved by the Board of Trustees.

E. Documentation of the required service hours (first renewal) or continuing education hours (subsequent renewals) must accompany the Renewal Application Form and may be verified by the appropriate member church Minister, or as designated by the Minister, the facilitator of continuing education work or the Practitioner Coordinator. Only the local church Minister may document satisfactory compliance with the basic renewal requirements as specified in Item B above.

F. If not renewed within the ninety (90) days, the license shall be declared inactive.

SECTION 2: CONTINUING EDUCATION UNITS

Any combination of CEU's totaling one hundred (100) every two years. At least three different categories of CEU's are required.

CATEGORY	UNITS
For Accredited UCRS Classes (Science of Mind Adult, Youth, Junior Church)	
Preparation for teaching	1 per class
Teaching	1 per class hour
Attendance at SOM classes (re-audit/assisting/aide)	1 per class hour
For Workshops or Seminars*	
Create and prepare final draft (confirmed by the minister)	10 units
Preparation for the presentation	1 per workshop hour
Presentation of the workshop	1 per workshop hour

Attendance at a workshop	1 per workshop hour
Non-Accredited Classes*	
Create and prepare final draft (confirmed by the minister)	10 units
Preparation for the presentation	1 per class hour
Presentation of the class	1 per class hour
Attendance at a class	1 per class hour
Published Materials (or accepted for publication)*	
Book	100 Units
Articles/SOM Magazine Meditations	25 Units
Professional Audio or Video Tape	100 Units
Attendance*	
Attendance at an activity that carries out items footnoted below	1 per each hour
Retreats/Educational Conferences	1 per each hour up to 25 per event
Active participation in Local Church Conference or convention Ministry of Prayer	1 per each hour
Ten minutes or more Sunday platform assistance per service	1 per each segment

Footnotes:

Additional CEUs may be earned by participation in activities deemed appropriate and valid by the Minister. Intent and purpose of CEU must be maintained.

Practitioners geographically separated from church and/or cities, may provide a write-up of tapes, videos of class materials from the Institute of

Religious Science, Asilomar speakers, or other appropriate seminars or workshops. This is to be cleared in advance with the Minister of the Practitioner's affiliate church.

* Discretion is advised. Workshops, seminars, classes and articles should promote the professional and the spiritual enhancement of the licensed Practitioner.

Chapter 29

Other Beliefs

A wide variety of spiritual practices and traditions are found in the world today. When looked at closely, many of them are based on core beliefs similar to Religious Science, but over time new interpretations and traditions have been added so that they often look dramatically different on the outside.

This section presents an overview of the major religions so that the Practitioner will have a basic idea of the various definitions of God that might be influencing the effect in the client's life.

Roman Catholicism

The Articles of Faith for Roman Catholics are found in The Apostles Creed and the Nicene Creed.

The Apostles Creed

I believe in God the Father Almighty, Maker of heaven
and earth, and in Jesus Christ, His only Son, our Lord,
Who was conceived by the Holy Ghost, born of the

> *Virgin Mary, suffered under Pontius Pilate, was crucified, died and was buried: He descended into hell: the third day He rose again from the dead. He ascended into heaven. And sitteth on the right hand of God the Father Almighty; from thence He shall come to judge the quick and the dead. I believe in the Holy Ghost, the holy Catholic Church: the Communion of saints, the forgiveness of sins; the resurrection of the body, and the life everlasting.*

We can see by this creed, God is the creator upon which all existence depends. The Church teaches that love is the highest quality that can be expressed in life and encourages total dedication to increasing the good in all areas of life. Since God is everywhere, each individual's life should be ruled by their relationship to God. In general, the Christian life is focused on becoming more Christ-like in daily life.

In Catholicism, attaining salvation is increased by individual confessions of sins and wrong doing in a confessional at the church and doing the penance (typically prayers) as instructed by the priest. Catholic beliefs include what is known as the Four Last Things: Death, Judgment, Hell (purgatory and resurrection of the body) and Heaven. Purgatory is that state where the soul goes at the time of death, when it has sins "on account" that have not been "paid for" through penance. Each person can shorten their time in purgatory by specific prayers and works, called indulgences. When the soul is cleansed, it enters into eternal union with God. It is believed that at the resurrection, the souls of all people will be reunited with their bodies.

The faith of Roman Catholics is faith in the infallibility of God and thus God's Church. In Church doctrine, the mediator between Christ and the individual soul is the Church. The individual only has a direct connection with Christ through prayer. The Church is the law and personal salvation is available only through the Church. St. Augustine clearly explained the strength of this belief when discussing the authority of the Church when he wrote "Rome has spoken. The matter is finished."

In this teaching scripture is seen as incomplete and requires the interpretation of the Church to get the correct understanding. To be a Roman Catholic means to have a commitment of faith in the reliability of the Catholic Church, which exists as the Body of Christ. The voice of the Church is accepted as the guiding voice of God and all other sources of truth are secondary. The scriptures are interpreted by the Church and if some experience or thing does not conform to the voice of the Church, it is invalid.

Protestantism

In historical context Protestantism is considered a fairly new religion since it is only about four centuries old. It is one of the three divisions of the Christian doctrine, along with the Roman Catholic and Orthodox Churches. Protestantism is unique in that it has hundreds of separate organizations, which have different beliefs and a wide variety of practices. Yet it is based on the belief that God deals directly with each person and salvation is achieved by faith alone. People are at the center of this branch of Christianity and are expected to express religious faith in their daily thoughts and actions. Although the basic beliefs and faith are the same, over time Protestantism has gained an incredible variety of appearances.

Protestant Christianity formed in the 15th and 16th centuries when some church leaders questioned the authority of the Catholic Church and the government in those countries where the church and government ruled everyday life. Martin Luther (1483-1546) is most often remembered. Instead of taking the word of the Church, these men created a new order where people were recognized as individuals, acting on their own personal authority and accepted responsibility for themselves. Protestants turned away from looking only to the Catholic Church for interpretation of the scriptures and began reading the bible and interpreting it individually.

They inferred that they had free will and were free spirits to choose their own idea of religious life. They felt a direct connection to God and no longer were willing to go through the Catholic Church as an intermediary.

As the Protestant movement solidified, scriptures became the infallible ruling document for life and individual spiritual practices—not the Church. Common to all of the Protestant factions were doctrines, which included belief in the Trinity, mankind as a sinner, the saving work of Christ and justification of acts by faith. The test of whether one was a Protestant Christian was one's adherence to these doctrines.

As knowledge and reasoning improved over time, conflicts arose between the conclusions reached by the use of reason vs. the doctrines of faith. For example, one such paradox is that some believed it was reasonable that people are natural creatures limited only by ignorance and lack of experience, while the scriptures indicated people were considered sinners. This contributed to a period in the 18th Century that was dominated by the use of reason in dealing with religious beliefs and was called the period of Rationalism. It was a new way of thinking that allowed biblical stories to be seen as stories and not accurate historical reports. This enabled Protestantism to be expressed and reflected in the day-to-day life of its members.

Today Protestant beliefs range from conservative to liberal (reason over doctrine) or fundamentalism (interpretation of doctrine) that have implications in the organization of the many churches and codes of conduct. At the core lies this basic thought, as related by the first Assembly of the World Council of Churches:

> *Christians are called to live responsibly, to live in response to God's act of redemption in Christ, in any society, even within the most unfavourable social structures.*

Judaism

Judaism is a religion with a rich history, most often remembered by the acts of God in the exodus of the Jewish people from Egypt. Jews embody the belief of being the chosen people whom God redeemed and their work is to keep His statutes as written in the Bible. This covenant is believed unbreakable.

The Jewish faith believes salvation is open to all people in any religion if they obey the law of righteousness—righteous conduct in imitating God's ways and being just and merciful. There is much emphasis on individual action. Life is seen as an arena of moral choices and each person can choose good.

The Hebrew Bible was written over a one thousand year time frame and was finished about 1000 AD. It is divided into three sections: The Torah (which includes the Five Books of Genesis), The Prophets, and The Writings. The Bible is a record of the Hebrew's understanding of God, His ways in relationship to the world and all people. It was written by many different scholars, yet contains some common assumptions: God's existence and power; the natural world as a manifestation of God's glory; views of God that range from a narrow concept of God as a national deity to a broad universal concept. God is seen as an imposing force demanding absolute obedience and also a loving and compassionate father who has a close relationship with those that honor him. Obedience to the Torah is the main focus of Judaism. The Mishnah is the code of Jewish law and is the second most sacred book.

Judaism believes there is one eternal God who created the universe and remains in control of it. God is omnipotent and all loving. He created humans as free agents with the ability to choose between good and evil. All people are created equal and should base their relationships with others on love, respect and understanding. The job of every person is to bring the light of divine unity to every act in daily life. Each person has an individual responsibility to society for its well-being, therefore there must be respect for government and its laws. Life is to be lived in piety and reverence before God and other people. The number one rule of conduct is the imitation of God. Communication with God is done through prayer and meditation. Prayers are a regular part of life and are done at specific times during the day and on special occasions.

In Jewish beliefs, suffering is never perceived as wasted. Its meaning or purpose is often believed to be hidden and beyond human understanding. Suffering is not seen as a direct punishment for sins or error, since it could be the result of sins of past generations. No doctrine of heaven or hell is found in Judaism, only the resurrection of the dead at the ultimate end. That is why living a loving and meaningful life each day is so important.

Buddhism

Buddhism is a religion based on insight as a means of conquering fear and elimination of suffering through realizing the true nature of things. It means "the Teachings of the Enlightened One." The practice is based on purification of conduct followed by purification of the mind, which leads to insight and right understanding. It makes it possible to give up grasping, clinging, infatuation and dependence on things.

Buddhism is generally thought of as following the way of life of The Awakened One, the Buddha Gotama, who lived about 80 years, around 566-486 BC. Its history covers about 120,000 years. When the Buddha talked to people, he spoke in parables, similes and anecdotes so the average person could identify with what he was explaining. When people choose to live on the path, it is believed that they will understand and appreciate the truth through personal experiences and verification of their faith.

The best way to understand the Buddhist doctrine is to practice it. What is known as the Three Fold Path includes morality, meditation, and wisdom, all done simultaneously. The Buddha's principle for life is to find the middle way between a life of extreme sensuality and luxury and extreme asceticism. The real Buddhism has no rites and rituals, manuals or books. It is the practice of the body, voice and mind working together against suffering. Every aspect is designed to bring knowledge.

The Noble Eightfold Path is both mental and physical. It includes: right understanding, knowledge of the practices of Buddhism; right aspiration, renunciation, benevolence and kindness; right speech, abstaining from lying, slander, and idle talk; right action, abstaining from taking what is not given; right livelihood, self support; right effort, positive uses of energy and will; right mindfulness, alert and not overcome with things of the world; right concentration, calm, sure, contemplative and aware.

Zen Buddhism

Zen Buddhism is only one of many forms of Buddhism and is the best known form in the west. It is not a teaching that comes from scriptures. It originated in China with roots in India. Zen was born during a talk by Buddha Shakyamuni when he declared to one of his disciples, "I have the most precious treasure, spiritual and transcendental, which this moment I hand over to you, O venerable Mahakashyapa." At this moment Mahakashyapa became enlightened. He took his new awareness out to the world and created what is known as Zen.

Around 520 AD a Zen master and Buddhist monk, Bodhidharma arrived in China from India, seeking refuge. He brought a special message that lit the fire of Zen throughout the country. He described Zen as "A special transmission outside the scriptures. No dependence upon words and letters; Direct pointing at the soul of man; Seeing into one's nature and the attainment of Buddhahood." Zen monks went from China to Japan in the 12th century. The word Zen was the Japanese pronunciation of Ch'an, meaning meditation. Here the practice of sitting in meditation became imbedded in Zen culture and practices. The Zen experience through meditation was then applied to the arts and lifestyles throughout society; the Zen experience was to do life in a meditative way.

Zen has none of the typical elements associated with religion. It is not a theology, but a religious path. American theologian and philosopher, Alan Watts, explained it this way:

> *Zen is a way and a view of life which does not belong to any of the formal categories of modern Western thought. It is not a religion or a philosophy; it is not a psychology nor a type of science. It is an example of what in India is known as a 'way of liberation,' and is similar in this respect to Yoga, Taoism, and Vedanta. A way of liberation can have no positive definition.*

Today Zen training has four main areas: Zazen, sitting in meditation; Koans, lessons or problems beyond logic that reduce reliance on form by using contradictions and paradox; Sanzen, private interviews with the master; Work, physical work that keeps one in contact with everyday life.

Taosim

Older than Confucious, the text of Taoism is called the Tao Te Ching and was written by Lao-tzu. He was born in 604 BC and wrote the text during a period of tremendous political and social unrest. Loa-tzu's beliefs were directly opposite to those of Confucious, who dedicated his life to imposing a moral system that would stop or eliminate the atrocities that had been going on for so long in their country. Lao Tzu wrote the doctrine of inaction or "not doing". This principle means that in human relationships force only defeats itself. Every action produces a reaction and every challenge has a response. As he explained, a bee being crushed will sting.

The Tao Te Ching gives only conclusions and does not lay out steps to be followed. Each individual must take the steps of right action on their own and the way they see it. This encourages an acceptance of universal harmony, accepting the natural cycles of life such as summer and winter, hot and cold, and Yin and Yang (which governs the behavior of all people.) Yin is the principle of darkness, cold and femininity and invites withdrawal, rest and passivity. Yang is the principle of light, heat and masculinity and invites activity, even aggression.

In the first or second century AD, the Tao was organized by one of its teachers into a religious structure with monasteries, temples, images, liturgies and rites, many of which persist until today.

Islam

The prophet Mohammed (born about 575 AD) founded this movement in the 7th Century in interior Arabia. Islam is an Arabic word meaning acceptance, surrender, submission, or commitment to a divine ruler whom they follow in every aspect of life. Those who practice Islam are called Muslims.

Islam is an inner attitude of recognizing ones obligations to fulfill the purpose of the Creator. Mohammed had visions from an angel and intense experiences of God some time after his 40th birthday. The visions showed him that his mission was to bring God's message to the people. He became a preacher, reformer and prophet in the city of Mecca for about ten years.

Mohammed's revelations and experiences over twenty years were recorded and are the core of the Muslim scripture, the Koran. His teachings focused on one sovereign deity, Allah, who controlled the destiny of all mankind. Allah created the universe, established its order and held mankind's fate in His hand. Initially Mohammed placed strong emphasis on the terror of judgment that awaited ungrateful people who refused submission to Allah. The Koran includes vivid accounts of the torments of hell.

The Koran shows Mohammed as a prophet whose purpose was to renew and restore spiritual guidance, not to create a new religion. This is reflected in the opening of the Koran, which is a prayer to God for guidance.

Today Muslim theology considers the Koran to be the very word of God and the highest authority in all matters of faith, theology and law. It contains warnings, it admonishes and instructs. The Koran teaches predestination and free will and at times emphasizes the necessity to choose whether to obey God. The unity of God is the most fundamental of Muslim beliefs. Next is free will, the freedom to choose and accept the consequences, punishment or reward. It is considered a tremendous act of piety to memorize the Koran.

Other Beliefs

QUESTIONS FOR DISCUSSION

Explain the Science of Mind principles: We believe in the eternal goodness, the eternal loving kindness and the eternal givingness of life to all. We believe in our own soul, our own spirit, and our own destiny. We understand that the life of man is God.

Chapter 30

Unity and Individuality

As you come to the end of this handbook and are ready to go forth and give yourself in service, are you comforted to know that enlightenment is an ongoing process? It is true, we never reach a place where our development stops; we are eternally evolving. But since we also know that God is all there is, in what way do we relate this to all of life's ups and downs? I think Ken Wilbur said it beautifully, "And so forms continue to arise, and you learn to surf."

Surfing is such a wild and exhilarating sport that requires intense concentration on the motion of the water and becoming one with it. Hard and fast, up and down, small and great, the waves of the ocean keep coming, just like life experiences. A surfer practices and develops strength and skills to work in harmony with the unpredictable nature of the ocean. Maintaining that sense of oneness takes focused effort and determination. With awareness and practice we, too, can hone our spiritual skills and surf harmoniously through life.

The Infinite never expresses itself in fragments. There is no such a thing as a part of God. In an indivisible unity, all of everything is present everywhere all the time.

Ernest Holmes

Inner peace and harmony comes from living in the knowledge of our oneness with God and all things. But there are times when we, as well as our clients, become hypnotized by our earthly experiences. We might inflate our own importance a little too much and it can be difficult to feel and see the unity around us. When we feel separate, our mind can be dominated by selfish urges, putting forth effort to have their own way to do only what we like, while we are unable to see at that moment, how we might help those around us. Jesus taught that we should not wait for a negative experience (a crash) to let go of our attachment to separateness, but to consciously turn away from those selfish needs and do something positive. By turning away from the darkness of separateness we walk into the light.

Light accompanies an expansion of consciousness. When we connect with our soul in deep meditation, we can see white light. If it could be seen with open eyes, affirmative prayer would be seen as a pathway of light. Holmes said, "This light is not created. It is not a psychological explosion; it is something which pre-exists." And in this illumination something is felt.

One way to see how perfectly both unity and individuality express in life is to observe rain. Eventually rainwater always returns to the ocean. Water may pause here or there in a lake or stream; it may evaporate into the clouds or be taken up by a thirsty plant; it may be the ice cubes that keep a glass of water cool. While water experiences its many forms, the ocean does not worry or fret—it just is. It waits patiently, knowing every drop of water is not lost, it is just on a journey of individual expression and will eventually find its way back into a stream, which eventually joins in perfect union with the ocean. All spiritual teachers have said we also eventually find our way back to a true recognition of oneness, our true nature. It may take some people longer than others—pausing as long as water frozen in a glacier—but at some point each one melts and finds their way back home.

Einstein expressed unity in his recognition of energy and mass being equal, identical, and interchangeable. The basis for metaphysics is the concept that there is no difference between the thought and what it does; there is no difference between the thought and the form it takes. How could thought change a form unless form were thought as form? It just couldn't. That is the whole basis of affirmative prayer. Just as an acorn becomes a tree, a solid thought creates the thing. How? Nobody knows, and it doesn't matter. What matters is that it happens. Holmes explains, "Then our aim is not to speak the right word, necessarily, but a word that is so completely accepted that it can operate." Do you remember a moment when you made a personal decision and it was so clear nothing was going to stop you? Determination and clarity are very powerful partners.

Dr. Raymond Charles Barker points this out in his book, *The Power of Decision.* He writes, "The universe is undisturbed by human stupidity and ignorance of what the individual really can be. The universe is never in a hurry. It is law and order. It waits for the individual to come to his senses and know himself aright. Once you know yourself as Mind, you forevermore control your experience through ideas, and not through the manipulation of material events." So are you ready? Where on your spiritual path have you been resting in eddies? Can you think of one small decision today that will move you forward? Knowing that the universe is behind you 100% and will support your decision to the degree you are clear and determined, what is one step you can take today towards what you want the most? Let affirmative prayer support this decision daily and watch the perfection unfold. It is the Law and it works.

When we are with friends and feel unity with the world, there is a sense of lightness in our body. Problems and worries fade into the distance. We intuitively know there is more to this life experience, it allows feelings of separateness to wash away. Scientists understand unity, because science has shown there is no energy that will destroy itself. We are dealing with One Mind, One Spirit, which expresses through thought, just as the thought of God expresses as all. Knowing how the Law of the Universe works, we can now focus on our thoughts while being consciously aware of the words we speak, because they will mold our life experience. Working with Law, we can now prove to ourselves that Law exists, so we thoroughly understand that our state of consciousness is in continuous creation.

"The great, the good, and the wise" have told us this 'thing,' this Divine essence is light, life, love, peace, power, beauty, and joy; divine attributes we can observe around us every day of the week. Troward describes these as attributes of Spirit, and as we contemplate each one, we become it. Spirit holds the possibility of everything and it resides in our individual consciousness. This Divine Mind is the field in which we plant our seeds; it is the field of eternal action. In each thing the Presence of God must exist as the idea **and the potentiality** of that thing in which it is incarnated. The potentiality of a tomato plant resides in the seed. How the seed received this identity is the process of evolution. "Within us must be the potential of everything we shall ever evolve into," writes Holmes. Just think of what has evolved over this past hundred years as a new century begins—computers, atomic war, airplanes, telephones, space stations... All of these things had the potential to exist many centuries ago—the potential was there, but it was the evolution of our thinking process, our knowledge and understanding, that put the pieces together to create a laptop computer.

> *Duplicity is a lie, the fundamental lie, the original untruthfulness—and the beginning of the 'small self,' the battered self, the self that hides its Original Face in the forms of its own suffering.*
>
> *Ken Wilber*

Evolution is a PRINCIPLE, which manifests in all form. It is the effect of Intelligence, not its cause. Evolution, the effect, only follows Involution, the idea. When we embody the idea, the form appears, which is why we believe behind everything is the movement of consciousness. Every idea we have is God expressing the Self. It is God's nature to know and crave expression. Every aspect of our life is Cause and Effect in action. Spirit Involves and Law Evolves mechanically. Evolution is an effect. Take a moment to look at your life and find the connection between: Involution…Evolution; Thought…Thing; Word…Law; Purpose…Execution.

Many sacred scriptures throughout the ages have taught unity and individuality. One text that focuses on spiritual self-mastery is the *Bhagavad Gita*. The epic stories found here are metaphors for the war between the forces of light and darkness in every person; the war between unity and individuality. In Chapter 2 of the text, spiritual teacher, Sri Krishna, reminds his student, Arjuna, of his immortal nature, the real Self that never dies, the eternal Self. The basic premise as Arjuna begins his path of spiritual awareness, is that the immortal soul is more important than the passing world. But Arjuna is told he will not fully realize this until he can see beyond the dualities of life and identify with the immortal Self through direct mystical experience. Krishna calls for disciplining the mind and detachment from dualities like pain and pleasure. The goal of the story is to teach that by expanding our spiritual awareness, our reaction to events will not be based on habit, but will be based on the freedom of non-attachment. Here again we find the power of the witness consciousness.

Krishna goes on to talk to Arjuna about attachment. "When you keep thinking about sense objects, attachment comes. Attachment can breed desire, the lust of possession that turns to anger. Anger clouds the judgment; you can no longer learn from past mistakes. Lost is the power to choose between what is wise and what is unwise; and your life is utter waste. But when you move amidst the world of sense, free from attachment and aversion alike, there comes the peace in which all sorrows end, and you live in the wisdom of the Self." When we enter this state of awareness, we feel bliss, then soon we again become aware of our body, our physical experience, and the sense of unity may fade like a dream. The moment we pierce the veil of illusion and touch infinity, our life changes. Consistent spiritual practices are the path to keep this channel of deep inner understanding open.

Heaven and hell are states of consciousness. We choose the degree to which we experience heaven or hell, because suffering is a conscious choice. Ernest Holmes believed that someday we will have learned all we need to through suffering and will decide that we've had enough. He believed we will reach this point through an evolutionary process and expressed it this way: "Evolution is the awakening of the soul to a recognition of its unity with the Whole." We will evolve into infinity. Behind evolution is an irresistible pressure compelling us to be more, better, higher, greater. We shall make progress, expanding in a sequence from where we are to whatever we shall become, forever spiraling upward. Evolution is what Troward and Holmes both believed begins with involution, where Spirit becomes matter, where we go within to become a conscious co-creator with God, which then evolves into higher and higher degrees of consciousness. Evolution is the process of Matter becoming Spirit—going back to our Oneness.

Mystics helped us to know that we, too, could reveal the Presence of God and have a deep spiritual perception. They didn't read our thoughts, but sensed the atmosphere of God. In our escalating abilities, we can hear and read about God, but the best knowledge is direct experience. The best method is to learn it for ourself, not second hand. What we experience is all we can know. Mother Teresa had a great gift of experiencing Jesus in everyone. She would say, "Each one is Jesus in His distressing disguise." How blissful that vision must be.

Conscious evolution progresses with things as simple as letting go of a belief in duality and recognizing that right and left, up and down, are just two sides of the same coin. The speed of our upward movement depends on how fast we let go of the negative beliefs we have carried around for a long time, such as blame or judgment. As we choose to be in a witness consciousness, where we are the observer, we see beyond labels of good and bad, inside and out, and know the truth about any situation. The freedom of sensing unity with everything makes it easier to let go of habits and patterns that don't serve us. Then we can trust in Spirit, let go of negativity knowing the Universe abhors a vacuum and will always fill it. The goal is to let go of the negative, be the observer, and know the Universe will fill us with love. Again, by letting go, our old habits will die from lack of attention.

By letting go, does this mean we won't have any more temptations? No. Like Ram Dass says, our ingrained habits never totally go away, but instead come back to us periodically like little schmoozes that tickle us, saying, "Are you really done with this one?" It makes me laugh, because when that happens I can really see how far I've progressed on letting go of that one! To me it's the ultimate cosmic giggle.

Getting into a witness consciousness in times of stress can be a challenging, but it is such a powerful tool. It offers us the optional perspective to think, "So this is my challenge," instead of getting drawn into the drama and negativity of a situation. As Practitioners, when we are in that clear space, we can see the play of consciousness in clients and then we can positively contribute to the situation with love. When we look at the ocean as a witness, that moment of pause gives us the feeling of oneness with the purity of the ocean, its rhythm and power, and the purity of our self. The sensation of being in the witness consciousness and the sensation we have when observing the ocean are the same. Unity is when we feel two sides of one experience, one reality. But so often we are not the witness and we don't feel Oneness. It is not that Oneness comes and goes, it is our understanding that comes and goes. Oneness just is. There has never been one second in all time when Oneness did not exist.

One of the shifts in my consciousness, after growing up Catholic and then finding Religious Science, was in discovering that Jesus was a mystic. There have been many mystics throughout the ages and they all agree that the soul is the pathway of self-discovery, where we find unity in all aspects of life. The great mystics like Jesus, Moses, Buddha, Mohammed, all talked with God and came to know God as "personal to those who believe in It's presence." They felt it is natural for us to turn to the Great Power behind everything. When we sincerely turn to God, not just in a time of need, we should get the sense of a Real Presence. In Religious Science we do this by turning within to find that place of inner peace and the recognition of God as our reality. With this knowing, our work as Practitioners is a tremendous gift to the consciousness of the world. Blessings to you.

Suggested Reading

Bailes, Dr. Fredrick, *Basic Principles of the Science of Mind*, DeVorss & Company 1971.

Bailes, Dr. Fredrick, *Your Mind Can Heal You*,

Barker, Raymond Charles, *The Power of Decision*, Dodd, Mead & Company, 1988.

Barker, Raymond Charles, *The Science of Successful Living*, DeVorss & Company 1957.

Barker, Raymond Charles, *Treat Yourself to Life*, Dodd, Mead & Company, 1991.

Bitzer, Robert, *Collected Essays of Robert Bitzer*, DeVorss & Company, 1990.

Butterworth, Eric, *The Universe is Calling*, HarperSanFrancisco, 1993.

Carlson, Richard, and Shield, Benjamin, *Healers on Healing*, Jeremy P. Tarcher, Inc. 1989.

Carter, Craig, *How To Use The Power of Mind*, Science of Mind Communications, 1991.

Carter, Craig, *Your Handbook for Healing*, Science of Mind Communications, 1961.

Dossey, Larry, *Healing Words*, HarperSanFrancisco, 1993.

Fox, Matthew, *Western Spirituality*, Bear & Company 1981.

Goldsmith, Joel, T*he Art of Spiritual Healing*, Harper Collins 1959.

Holmes, Ernest, *Living the Science of Mind*, DeVorss & Company, 1991.

Holmes, Ernest, and Kinnear, Willis, *Practical Application of Science of Mind*, Science of Mind Publications, 1987

Holmes, Ernest, *The Anatomy of Healing Prayer*, Holmes Papers Volume 2, DeVorss & Company 1992.

Holmes, Ernest, *The Holmes Papers Volume I*, South Bay Church of Religious Science 1989.

Holmes, Ernest, *The Science of Mind*, G.P. Putnam & Sons, 1966.

Holmes, Ernest, *Living The Science of Mind*, DeVorss & Company, 1984.

Hopkins, Emma Curtis, *Scientific Christian Mental Practice*, High Watch Fellowship 1958.

Ingraham, E.V., *Wells of Abundance*, DeVorss & Company 1966.

Schultz, J. Kennedy, *A Legacy of Truth*, Brob House Books 1987.

Troward, Thomas, *The Edinburgh Lectures & Dore Lectures on Mental Practice*, DeVorss & Company, 1989.

Troward, Thomas, *The Law And The Word*, Dodd, Mead & Company, 1917.

Troward, Thomas, *Bible Mystery And Bible Meaning*, G.P. Putnam's Sons, 1988.

About the Authors

Mary Schroeder, began studying *The Science of Mind* under the leadership of Dr. James and Dr. Andrea Golden in Redding, California in 1990 and has been a Licensed Practitioner with the Redding Church of Religious Science since 1993. She completed Fourth Year ministerial studies in 1998. Currently Mary is in a training program in Pastoral Care at a local hospital. She has a degree in Forest Industries Management from The Ohio State University and works as the District Manager of the local Resource Conservation District, which specializes in fisheries and wildlife habitat restoration projects.

Dr. James Golden and Dr. Andrea Golden, have been pastors of the Redding Church of Religious Science since 1986. Many of their students have gone on to be very successful pastors and practitioners at other churches around the country. Dr. James uses the principles of Science of Mind in challenging his congregants to step out of their day-to-day comfort zones and express life in new ways. Through skydiving, white water rafting, and wilderness adventures, Dr. James leads his students to new levels of empowerment by breaking through mental, spiritual and physical boundaries. His popular weekly television show, *Principles For Successful Living*, is seen throughout the northern California area. Dr. James also serves as a chaplain with the Redding Police Department and is on the Ethics Board at Redding Medical Center.

0-595-20687-5

Printed in the United States
38335LVS00006B/61-129